Both the publishing industry *have become so fragmented that just the idea of trying to navigate them can totally paralyze a new author. In "Make A Big Impact," Melanie Herschorn has written an accessible, confidence-boosting step-by-step approach that will help authors get their books into people's hands, and their ideas into reader's minds.*

~ Scott Detrow, weekend host of All Things Considered and a co-host of the Consider This podcast at NPR

Writing a compelling book is only part of the journey, reaching the right audience is equally crucial. Melanie Herschorn brilliantly unveils the secrets to long-term success in her debut book. Her wisdom on author marketing strategies is a much needed life-line for writers illuminating the path to literary triumph and leaving an unforgettable mark on the world of storytelling.

~ Ann Gurrola, President/Owner Elevate Publicity & Marketing, Los Angeles

Melanie Herschorn shares invaluable insights in her book, offering writers a roadmap to navigate the complex world of promotion. With her guidance, writers can embark on a path to enduring success, where her stories will resonate with readers for years to come.

~ Marleah Leslie, President/Owner, Marleah Leslie & Associates – Publicity and Marketing

My first book was the catalyst for the thriving community and business I have today, so I know firsthand how vital the marketing component of a book launch is! Melanie Herschorn's new book "Make A Big Impact With Your Book" is exactly what new authors need to ensure that their books have longevity and make a real difference.

~ Lindsey Schwartz, Founder, Powerhouse Women

Melanie Herschorn guides readers through the daunting task of book marketing with the wit and easygoing nature of a best friend. This is not only a wonderful resource, but it's a breeze to read and a terrific inspiration. Time for me to write a book, just so I can put these lessons into action!

~ Ben Mandelker, co-host of the Watch What Crappens podcast which earns over 3 million listens a month and has been a fixture in iTunes' Top 10 for TV & Film podcasts.

MAKE A
BIG
IMPACT
WITH YOUR BOOK

MAKE A
BIG
IMPACT
WITH YOUR BOOK

AUTHOR MARKETING STRATEGIES
FOR LONG-TERM SUCCESS

MELANIE HERSCHORN

Make a Big Impact with Your Book: Author Marketing Strategies for Long-Term Success
Published by Mission Possible Media
Phoenix, Arizona, U.S.A.

HERSCHORN, MELANIE, Author
MAKE A BIG IMPACT WITH YOUR BOOK
MELANIE HERSCHORN

Library of Congress Control Number: 2023915902
ISBN: 979-8-9887947-0-7, 979-8-9887947-1-4 paperback
ISBN: 979-8-9887947-2-1 hardcover
ISBN: 979-8-9887947-3-8 digital

BUSINESS & ECONOMICS / E-Commerce / Digital Marketing
BUSINESS & ECONOMICS / Industries / Media & Communications
BUSINESS & ECONOMICS / Women in Business

Editing: Karen Hunsanger (karenhunsanger.com)
Proofreading: Catherine Turner (turnerproofreading.com)
Book Design: Dino Marino (dinomarinodesign.com)
Book Coaching: Susie Schaefer (finishthebookpublishing.com)

QUANTITY PURCHASES: Schools, companies, professional groups, clubs, and other organizations may qualify for special terms when ordering quantities of this title.
For information, email hello@vipbookmarketing.com.

MISSION
POSSIBLE
MEDIA ™

DEDICATION

For Deanna and Nicholas, the two brilliant minds who
challenge me every day.
And for Helen, my beautiful grandma who has shown me
how to live a life of meaning.

TABLE OF CONTENTS

SPECIAL INVITATION

Imagine, for a moment, what it would be like if you could develop a sustainable way to get your book into the hands of your dream audience.

You will be on your way to becoming a thought leader in your space and making an impact with your book.

Thought leaders are mission-driven self-starters who know a book can help them land paid speaking engagements, make regular book sales, and generate leads who are ready to be part of their brand and mission . . .

So, if this sounds like you, you're in the right place.

As an author, you have important expertise and a unique message. But without a clear road map to share that message and build a community around your mission, it can be tough to get your audience to buy your book, let alone propel your business forward.

To help you create your personal book marketing plan, here is a free resource to begin sharing your book with the world. Download the Ultimate Book Marketing Checklist here: vipbookmarketing.com/checklist.

INTRODUCTION

Whether it has taken you a weekend or a decade to write your book, you are in the right place. Congratulations! *You are an author.*

If you are anything like me, it may have been your lifelong dream to publish a book. In the fourth grade, I *attempted* to write a Young Adult (YA) novel with a friend of mine. The premise was similar to that of a Judy Blume book I adored at the time, and I think each chapter was the length of one side of a blue-lined, loose-leaf page. Those pages are long gone now, but I will never forget the feeling of pride I felt for writing what I thought was the greatest book a 10-year-old could ever dream up.

Back in the 1980s, I had no idea how to get it published (Amazon was still just a rainforest in those days), but I believed my work was totally worthy. My hope for you is that you are feeling just as proud as that fourth grader—that you have congratulated yourself for accomplishing something most people will only ever talk about but never actually get around to finishing.

I also hope that you have had a bit of time to get reacquainted with yourself *now that you are an author.*

> **Look in the mirror and say it out loud.**
> **I'm (your name goes here), and I am an author!**

Not everyone has what it takes—the discipline, the drive, the stick-to-itiveness—to get published. But you do. Before we go any further, I want to make sure that you get the most out of our time together. Head to vipbookmarketing.com to get bonus materials and so much more to help you on your book marketing journey.

THE CURRENT PUBLISHING LANDSCAPE

With more publishing options available than ever before, there has been a leveling of the playing field for would-be authors. Those who may not have historically been able to secure a book deal with a traditional publisher can opt for self-publishing or hybrid publishing instead. Although the book may not end up on the *New York Times* Best Sellers List, *every* author has the opportunity to sell their books on Amazon or Barnes and Noble.

Both traditionally published authors and those who have chosen the hybrid or self-publishing model are also on a level playing field when it comes to marketing their books. Every author has the power to build their own author platform—the foundational marketing that enables you, as an author and, therefore, a brand, to establish your credibility and authority online through social media, email marketing, podcasting, and so much more. And it isn't just that you have the power to do this; it is really the prerequisite for your book's success. In fact, traditional publishers expect new authors to have an established community of raving fans prior to the date the book drops, or at least be well on their way to growing that community, and it is up to the author to build it, not the publisher.

WHY IT TAKES A VILLAGE

It is easy for an author to get so wrapped up in the writing, editing, and publishing process that by the time the book is ready for purchase, they are burned out and have spent all their allotted book budget on production with no money left for marketing. I see this happen way too often. Then the author is faced with a big dilemma: How are they supposed to get their book into the hands of their ideal readers without an effective marketing plan? Inevitably, the author will try something—hire a company that gets them on a bunch of podcasts with no return on investment or post umpteen photos of them with their book on social media—hoping it garners sales. But when none of their haphazard marketing attempts move the needle, they give up and move on, leaving a stack of books to collect dust.

I am on a one-woman mission to end this silliness. Just like you would not plan a big birthday party, choose a fabulous venue, a top-notch caterer, fun decorations, and the perfect outfit, and then not send out any invitations to guests, you shouldn't publish a book and then not tell anyone about it in a way that sells books (your marketing).

Here is another way to think about it. You have spent countless hours creating your book. It is like birthing a baby— the baby that you have dreamed of having. Even if you opted to write your book in a shorter amount of time or gathered already written blog posts or podcasts to fill the pages, it still takes tons of brainpower, organization, and stamina.

Heck, even if you hired a ghostwriter to actually write the book, you still had to recount it all to them and make sure it sounded like you and conveyed your message.

When a baby is born, its parents become literally obsessed with it, taking a million photos and filling up their social media feeds with an endless barrage of pics of the cutest baby they have ever seen. We are not snakes. We do not slither off, leaving our young to fend for themselves. We give our innocent little babies everything we can to help them be happy, well-adjusted, and healthy. We also say that it takes a village to raise a child.

Like that human baby, when your book arrives, you need to nurture it to grow and raise it so that it can make a difference in the world. You want to get it into the hands of everyone who will benefit from reading it. That takes a village too!

> *"There will come a time when you believe everything is finished; that will be the beginning."*
>
> ~ Louis L'Amour

DOESN'T WRITING A BOOK MEAN YOU ARE A THOUGHT LEADER?

A common misconception is that writing a book automatically makes you a thought leader. FACT: It does not, especially if no one knows about the book. While it is absolutely true that when you write a book based on your work, you have free rein to tell people what you do and how you help clients, and then to mention, "...and I wrote the book on it." Your book does not, however, give you license to tell people that you are a thought leader.

> Telling people you are a thought leader
> will not make you a thought leader.
> Others must bestow that title upon you.

4

According to Denise Brosseau, the author of *Ready to Be a Thought Leader* and founder of the Thought Leadership Lab, thought leaders are defined as:

"Informed opinion leaders and the go-to people in their field of expertise. They become the trusted sources who move and inspire people with innovative ideas, turn ideas into reality, and know and show how to replicate their success. Over time, they create a dedicated group of friends, fans and followers to help them replicate and scale their ideas into sustainable change not just in one company but in an industry, niche or across an entire ecosystem."[1]

So, if you are ready to step into thought leadership, then you are in the right place! With strategic and consistent marketing of your book and your brand, you will step into the "go-to expert" space and become known as the authority in your field. That is why I am so glad you are here.

YOUR MISSION IS POSSIBLE

Why take my word for it? Because I have helped hundreds of authors with their messaging, positioning, and marketing strategy and tactics to build communities of raving fans with marketing that truly resonates with their ideal readers. And that is literally my mission, what gets me out of bed every day. I get to help authors, just like you, amplify their authority to make this world a better place.

My route to get here was rather nonlinear, though. When I graduated from college, I ran away from Canada to Los Angeles to work in Hollywood. I spent a few years writing press releases, walking red carpets with celebrities, and hanging out backstage at notable talk shows. But I yearned for more and headed back to school at age 26 for a master's degree in broadcast journalism. My first job out of graduate school was working as an afternoon news anchor and general assignment reporter at a radio news station in central Pennsylvania. I was the only woman in a newsroom of men and felt like a fish out of water coming from LA to a small city of just 50,000 people.

At radio station-sponsored events, which I was obligated to attend, I would often get backhanded compliments from guests (read: big donors) like, *"You're sounding a bit better"* or *"You don't sound as new anymore,"* and sometimes outright insults about me and my reporting. At least no one ever told me I had a face for radio! Whenever I misspoke live on the air, my news director would come running toward me from the newsroom, ready to reprimand me. Since the entire radio booth was glass, I knew ahead of time when I was about to "get it."

With such constant scrutiny (one senator's campaign manager spent 20 minutes screaming at me over a misunderstanding), I developed a pretty thick skin.

> **I soon stopped worrying about what other people thought of me because I realized that no matter what I did, I could not please everyone.**

Armed with that protective shell, I decided to pursue a new purpose: to tell the stories of those whose voices deserved to be heard. While I still covered the stories assigned to me, whenever my news director gave me an inch of freedom, I would highlight issues about women, children, veterans, and older people, doing my best to give them a voice on our airwaves.

Some of the in-depth reports included stories such as a story on a camp for young children who had lost a parent or sibling, a series on the wives of senatorial candidates, and a three-part story on teens stuck in the Pennsylvania foster care system. I'm proud to say that these stories garnered journalism awards, but the most rewarding part was the gratitude from those featured in the stories.

Around my second year at the station, my husband and I started talking about having children. I knew that having a baby would be frowned upon, so we waited to start trying until a nonelection year. I reasoned that at least my three-month maternity leave would not interfere with election reporting. When I was five months pregnant with my first child, I was abruptly laid off from the station. At that point in my life, my entire identity had been wrapped up in being a journalist, and without that position, I felt like I was nothing. What's more, reporters from other news outlets began calling me to ask why I had been laid off so they could include it in their outlets. I had become the story.

As luck would have it, I was not unemployed for long. The local newspaper scooped me up and brought me on to cover an inner-city school district with serious budgetary woes. So, I still got to report and give a voice to the voiceless.

When my daughter was about eight months old, we moved to Arizona. I knew that any job in journalism would pay me less than I would be paying for childcare, so I opted to answer the call of entrepreneurship, which had been tapping on my heart really loudly. Within a year, I launched a line of breastfeeding shirts and dresses for nursing moms. Not really a normal trajectory, I know. Still, I single-handedly grew the brand, and within a few years, my products were being sold in boutiques across North America, on Amazon, and on Nordstrom's website.

My favorite part of the business was marketing, and I really wanted to get better at it. So, I hired a woman I knew who claimed to be an internet marketing expert who could help me make my brand a household name. Unfortunately, that was the beginning of the end of my company. She became verbally and emotionally abusive toward me, constantly telling me that my ideas were boring and that there was no way I could ever do the marketing myself. *"How is it that you have a master's degree in journalism?"* she would ask. You might be thinking, *But Melanie, you hired her . . . you could have severed ties at any time.* This woman had me believing that not only did I need her, but that there would also be repercussions if I tried to sever our working relationship. Over the course of a year, I paid her upward of $25,000.

When it was finally over, I had

- grown my Instagram following by about 5,000 followers with people who never had and were never going to buy what I was selling
- the belief that everything I wrote was boring and that I was not smart enough to do marketing for my business without her
- experiences of verbal and emotional abuse that made me too fearful to stand up for myself in case she tried to do a smear campaign against my company

I could not even go into my home office anymore. I shut down the business shortly thereafter.

After some serious introspection and talking with friends, I resolved to turn that awful experience into something positive. I found my voice and my mission again. When I looked back at my career up to that point, I saw that I had truly developed a skill set to support business owners with their marketing. I also tallied that I had logged about 10,000 hours of marketing, a figure that author Malcolm Gladwell has made famous in his book *Outliers: The Story of Success* as the number of hours it takes to achieve world-class expertise at a particular skill.[2] When I originally opened my current company, my goal was to ensure that other business owners would stop being misled by marketers making all sorts of promises. Over time, the mission has evolved to focus solely on helping authors to amplify their voices.

THE AUTHOR-MARKETER

As you read through this book, you will learn what it takes to create thought-leader content and messaging that resonates with *your* ideal readers. You will discover what authors often get wrong with their marketing and gain clarity on how to make sure that *you* are in the driver's seat when marketing your book.

> **You likely didn't know that in addition to "author," you'd also have to be "marketer." You are not alone.**

You may be thinking, *But Melanie, I'm not a marketer. I'm a (fill in your profession), and that's why I wrote the book on it.* As an author, you are truly your best marketer. When you talk about why you have written your book, when you tell stories about your past and how you have helped transform the lives of others through your work, you get attention.

Nobody is born knowing how to market their book. It is not your fault that when you spend all this time writing and editing, and likely pay *a lot* of money to publish it, no one has told you that publishing is just the beginning. I regularly hear from authors who were led to believe that simply publishing a book would give them the credibility they desire. They pretty quickly realize that no one knows about their book and that it is not doing what they were promised it would. I also hear from authors who wrote a book a year or two ago. They had a successful bestseller campaign but were never able to sell as many copies of their book as they had hoped to after becoming a bestseller. Now their published work sits alongside its identical cousins—sometimes hundreds of them—in a box or a closet, collecting dust.

The good news is, this does not have to be your book's fate. Unlike a carton of milk, your book does not expire. Sure, ideas may need to be reworked into a second edition, but the overarching themes and stories endure. You can (and should!) continue to market your book well after its launch. There are always new ways to create excitement about it. The more eyes you get on your book, thanks to your marketing, the more readers you will reach.

So, if this is you

- You are throwing the proverbial spaghetti at the wall to see what sticks (and not much does).
- You feel like you are wasting time and throwing good money after bad.
- You are frustrated and in need of clarity. (You have written the book, now what?)

I want you to imagine this instead:

- You have clear messaging that you know resonates with and inspires your ideal audience.
- You have a plan for your email marketing and social media and the know-how to execute it.
- You are growing a community of loyal followers who are so excited to buy your book.

When you provide value to your online audience, you show them that you are the go-to expert in your industry. Your content marketing will help you grow a community of ideal readers who become raving fans when they get to know, like, and trust you. This book can help you get there.

Take a moment to think of books that have made an impression on you and have had a big impact on your life or career. How did the stories and lessons in these books resonate with you or help you experience an important transformation?

One book that has greatly inspired me in my entrepreneurial journey is *The Go-Giver,* from authors Bob Burg and John David Mann. It's a parable that illustrates the importance of integrity and giving. It is one of the books I keep close by so I can refer back often.

Your book has the power to change lives, too. Now let's talk about your mission.

What some of our happy authors have to say:

After I completed writing draft three of my book (and although a marketer by profession), I had no idea what was required to improve my visibility among potential readers and to grab the attention of agents and publishers. In a period of six months, Melanie taught me everything I needed to know to elevate both my personal brand and my book. Melanie is like a human encyclopedia when it comes to book marketing, and she's shown tremendous value to me through her services. I highly recommend working with Melanie if you are in need of comprehensive book marketing.

~ **Laurie B. Timms,** Author

"Melanie is an intuitive marketer who specializes in Digital Marketing platforms for authors. In addition to helping expertly position me as an authoritative self-publishing author on the web, her years in broadcast media, journalism and experience in traditional marketing methods are what truly sets her apart in an industry often bogged down by amateur marketers who merely push the technical aspects of web marketing without the strategy and execution. Together, we recently successfully funded a $16K Kickstarter campaign in 31 days—an accomplishment that would have been impossible for me without a solid digital presence she helped me create. Her input at every single step of the way (from messaging to blind surveys to target audience interviews and even script writing) is why I would unequivocally choose Melanie as a marketing partner for success from start to finish. In addition, my confidence as an author and businesswoman has increased tenfold from Melanie's support and coaching. The sky is the limit for you when you invest in yourself by hiring Melanie to build your business strategically from the ground up.

~ **Lin Hawthorne,** Author and Publisher

I began working with Melanie in the spring of 2022 before my book came out. Her counsel was one of the key reasons it became an Amazon Best Seller. Now we are in November of 2022, and I just committed to an ongoing relationship where we consult any time I have questions about what I am doing. I now refer to her as my consigliere, my Devil's Advocate, and an inspiration. While I am actively involved every day with offshoots of my book—speaking engagements, blogs, podcasts, and the like, there is nothing quite as cathartic as a conversation with Melanie. She tells me when I have an awful idea—kindly—and she gets excited when there are breakthroughs. She is truly a partner in my success.

~ **Michael Ross,** Author and Financial Advisor

Melanie is an incredibly knowledgeable and insightful guide through the overwhelming and confusing realm of book and brand promotion and marketing. I am a longtime professional writer and first-time author in the process of launching my first book. Most people probably think that writing the book is the biggest challenge, but I quickly learned that what you do with the book after it's written is where the real adventure is. Melanie was able to help me identify the important content pillars in my work, coach me on how to leverage those pieces in my promotion and opened my mind up to a whole new world of possibilities establishing a brand and a voice. She is a delight to work with and I left our session inspired and energized with a much greater understanding that my book is just a part of what I'm promoting, and just a piece in a much bigger picture. If you're an author looking for help establishing and promoting your message, I can't recommend Melanie and VIP Book Marketing enough.

~ **Jim Schneider,** Author

CHAPTER 1

IT STARTS WITH YOUR MISSION

Uncovering your real mission may not be easy. But wow, is it worth it.

As I mentioned in the introduction, after closing down my clothing company of seven years, I was staring at a crossroads. But I was not sure what to do next.

> Once an entrepreneur, always an entrepreneur, so I could not picture myself working for someone else.

Around that time, a few different people had reached out to me to ask for business advice. After spending hours giving away tons of suggestions about marketing, branding, and the logistics of setting up a company, it hit me: people might actually pay me to do this.

Eventually, I mustered the courage to ask for money in return for my consulting, and my new business was born. But every time I was on a Zoom call with other entrepreneurs or was interviewed on a podcast, someone would ask, "What's your why?" I'd stumble over an answer.

I had always thought "my why" had to be some fiery catastrophe from which I'd bounced back even better, like a phoenix rising from the ashes. Surely, a near-death experience or someone else's near-death experience could be the only thing to differentiate me and be the "why." But I am happy to report that it is not necessary to *almost* take a long walk off a short cliff to locate your mission for your book, your business, and your brand as a whole. In fact, your mission may even be hiding in plain sight. Mine was.

Connecting with and staying connected to your bigger mission in the world is vital. In his book *Start with Why: How Great Leaders Inspire Everyone to Take Action*, Simon Sinek[3] sums it up beautifully:

"Very few people or companies can clearly articulate WHY they do WHAT they do...By WHY, I mean what is your purpose, cause or belief? WHY does your company exist? WHY do you get out of bed every morning? And WHY should anyone care?"

Remember that "marketing guru" I hired? When I finally cut ties with her, it took me a few months to get through the fog of that extremely stressful time. But I made a promise to myself that I would never let something like that happen again, to me or to any other unsuspecting business owners. *Not on my watch.* It also made me determined not to let one more entrepreneur spend so much money on hiring someone to do the work for them without first understanding it themselves.

Then I opened my current business, VIP Book Marketing, and promptly pushed that whole incident out of my mind because it was just too uncomfortable to relive. At networking events, if I was asked what I do and why I do it—every networking event—I gave really superficial answers. To be honest, for a while, I did not even realize that my experiences with that woman were even related to my work now. I compartmentalized very well. But one day, during a live workshop for about 50 people, it all came pouring out of me (tears too).

After I ended that live video, I was shaking. But I also felt strangely free. I began owning my "why" story. And you can too. Now you see, not every mission has to be caused by a front-page news headline. I have taken what I believe is my purpose on this planet—to help amplify authors' voices as they work to make this world a better place—and realized that this is the mission of my brand. Because I believe deep in my soul that there should be more goodness in the world, and the best way to make that happen is to help get authors' thoughts and ideas out in the online space as a guide who is supportive and an advocate.

"How do you know if your mission in life is finished? If you're still alive, it isn't."
~ Richard Bach

The authors we work with are on a mission, perhaps in their small way, to put their unique touch on the world and to make life easier and better for others. Often when we begin working together, my clients need to get a bit more clarity on their mission, so that is where we start.

YOUR MISSION CAN BEGIN IN CHILDHOOD

Take my client Lynsi, for example, who teaches and practices hypnosis for women who are trying to conceive. Through her work, she has helped hundreds of babies come into this world and made the dreams of countless women come true.

In our first meeting, I asked her what her mission was. Her initial answer was "to help get women pregnant."

We then went further.

A quick note, as a trained journalist, I'm not usually happy with the first answer because that is often the easy one. I like to really get to the meat of the issue. That is where the humanity lies. As we kept chatting, we got to the crux of it:

As a young girl, Lynsi felt distressed by the thought that women who wanted babies may not be able to have them. This deep-seated worry came to her mind a lot. When she was nine years old, she heard an announcement on the radio that made an indelible impact on her. Louise Joy Brown, the first baby born through in vitro fertilization,[4] had arrived safely into the world. At that moment, Lynsi recalls thinking to herself, *Now, no woman will ever have to be without a baby if she wants one.* At the time, she believed it was as though her prayers had been answered. Although she later learned that the scientific breakthrough would not be a silver bullet for every woman, that seemingly small moment had immense power and became a crucial piece in her creation of HypnoFertility.

> **Your life experiences shape your choices, and you may feel called to something even if you are unable to articulate why at first.**

PEEL BACK MORE LAYERS TO DISCOVER YOUR TRUE MISSION

My client Kim has a successful real estate business, and she specializes in helping her clients not only find their dream home but also determine that the home will fill their soul. At first, when we spoke about her mission for her book, she told me that she wants to help women get real with themselves, determine who they are at the core, and then show them how to live more meaningfully, starting with where they actually live.

I tend to be a straight shooter, and I will tell someone point-blank: "I know there is more." I always mean it from a place of love and respect, but it is important to expose what lies beneath.

Helping women reach their potential is a great thing. But there is more. That *more* is what differentiates you. It is what makes you stand out from your competition. Upon more reflection, Kim told me about her ability to see people's potential even when they cannot see it. She then revealed that she felt like she had missed out on 30 years of her own life, having failed to express her own views and gifts while in the wrong career, the wrong marriage, and the wrong home. As a former people pleaser, she is now on a mission to shorten the journey for others and clear a path for them to live happily. And then we had it, her real mission. When you have a mission, it is almost tangible. You can feel it in your bones. It is a driving force for your work and the reason you write a book. You want to sprinkle that magic around.

Have you really dug down deep to declare your mission to yourself and others?

I'm going to be the first to tell you that it is not always simple to figure it out for yourself. Heck, if I had not shared that embarrassing story in the middle of a live video, I do not know how long it would have taken me to peel away the layers of my mission.

So, what happens if you cannot seem to decipher what your mission is?

You now know it does not have to be something traumatic that happened in childhood. No escaping an explosion or dodging an asteroid.

In my work as a journalist, my goal was to help people tell their stories and just be the conduit for those stories. That has helped me tremendously with getting to the root of my clients' "why."

Here are some questions to ask yourself to get clear on your mission:

- How do I help my clients?
- What gets me out of bed in the morning?
- Why am I writing/why did I write a book?
- What do I want to achieve when someone reads my book?
- What ultimately drives me?
- What are my top five values?
- What do I want to be known for?
- What do I want to do to leave this world better than when I got here?

WHAT ABOUT MONEY? WHAT ABOUT FAME? CAN THOSE BE YOUR MISSION?

I'm going to say no, but also yes.

It's rare to find a human who doesn't have money blocks to work through. I credit Denise Duffield-Thomas and her book *Get Rich, Lucky Bitch!: Release Your Money Blocks and Live a First-Class Life* with giving me amazing insights into this.[5] It is fantastic to want to make lots of money. Maybe you want to buy a beach house, take a trip around the world, retire your spouse, drive a Ferrari . . . I completely support you in your goals. You want to see your name in lights, on a billboard in Times Square, be a guest on Oprah's latest show . . .

But at the end of the day, these things really are not actually your "why." They do not have the ability to keep you going the way your real mission will. I invite you to take some time now to uncover why you really do what you do so you can grow an audience of raving fans who will get on board with your mission and be thrilled to buy your book, watch you speak on stage, and so much more.

Now I want to invite you to head to vipbookmarketing.com for even more resources to help you market your book. Each chapter has bonus materials, so be sure to check it out!

KEY TAKEAWAYS

- Your mission doesn't have to be a catastrophic event. It can be a small thing that inspired you—small moments can hold great power.

- Your mission may be hidden in plain sight. You just need to start peeling back the layers to uncover it.

- You do have a mission, and there are no wrong answers.

- Ask yourself: What do I hope to achieve with my book?

- Money and fame can certainly be a driving force, but they are not as rooted as your mission.

QUESTIONS FOR REFLECTION

- How do I help my clients?

- What gets me out of bed in the morning?

- Why am I writing this book?

- What do I want to achieve when someone reads my book?

- What ultimately drives me?

- What are my top five values?

- What do I want to be known for?

- What do I want to do to leave this world better than when I got here?

CHAPTER 2

WHAT IS CONTENT MARKETING?

The book-writing process is not for the faint of heart. Whether you have written your book in 90 days or 90 months, or chosen whether to self-publish, work with a hybrid publishing company, or pitch your book to agents and traditional publishers, all the effort that goes into publishing your book is enough to make your head spin. Add in what it takes to become an Amazon best-selling author or to get a PR campaign together for a media blitz when you launch; it is exhausting.

But none of this hard work yields a long-lasting impact on your book.

Kevin Costner's baseball movie from the 1980s, Field of Dreams, is about a man who hears a voice telling him to build a baseball diamond in a cornfield. The voice says, "If you build it, he will come." That movie echoes what so many business owners, coaches, consultants, and speakers believe to be true:

> **If you write the book, the opportunities and sales will come. Thank you, Hollywood, but that is not really how things work in the real world.**

The vital piece absent from the aforementioned publishing process is creating your online presence and building your authority with an audience of raving fans—even before your book is launched. How do you do this? With a robust content marketing strategy.

DESIGN YOUR CONTENT MARKETING STRATEGY

When you have written your book and are seeking the most strategic way to share information about it to inspire your ideal readers to buy the book, you need a content marketing strategy. If you do not have a growing community of fans online, regular social media posts, and email campaigns that attract and nurture your ideal audience, who are you going to sell your book to? You want to get eyes on your book and your brand. And the way to do that is to create content that shines.

This is really, really, *really* important:

More and more, publishers of all kinds are stepping away from the marketing piece. In fact, I've heard it said that traditional publishers only roll out the red carpet two feet, and then authors are on their own. But these publishers still expect authors to have a loyal online following and a marketing plan in place. This can be terribly overwhelming to someone who thought writing the book was the tough part and that the rest would be a breeze. Authors who opt to go the hybrid or self-publishing route may be expecting to take on the marketing for themselves, but I still so often see them blindsided by what marketing a book truly requires.

It is really difficult to get rich from book sales alone. Authors like James Patterson, Danielle Steel, and John Grisham have done it, but they are not the norm. Steve Piersanti, the founder of Berrett-Koehler Publishers, has written about the state of publishing and notes that the average book has less than a 1 percent chance of being stocked in a typical bookstore. He also says that authors, not publishers, do most book marketing, and books tend to sell more to the authors' and publishers' communities than to the average reader at large.[6] I am not sharing this to discourage you, though. Instead, I want you to feel inspired. Piersanti's comments underscore what you now already know: The onus is on you to create an online presence that is filled with value and positions you as an authority so that you can grow a community of raving fans who want to buy your books. This knowledge puts you ahead of the competition.

"Most book marketing is done by authors, not publishers."
~ Steve Piersanti, Founder of Berrett-Koehler Publishers

HOW CAN AUTHORS MAKE MONEY IN REAL LIFE?

I am not a gambler, but even if I were, you and I both know the odds of becoming the next J. K. Rowling with your nonfiction book that highlights your expertise or your children's book that teaches kids patience are not great. But you *can* make money by leveraging your book as part of your marketing. International best-selling author and *HuffPost* contributor BJ Gallagher says it beautifully in an article for *HuffPost:* "Writing and publishing a book makes you an 'expert' without having a Ph.D. or university affiliation. Even if you lose money on the book, it can still be worth it in terms of increasing your fees, building your client base, selling more of whatever your product is, and building a name for yourself in your chosen field."[7]

There should be no shame in shouting from the rooftops how amazing you are for becoming an author and sharing your gifts with the people you want to help, especially since the statistics floated in writers' circles are that 97 percent of writers never finish their books.[8] If you have beaten the odds and published a book, no matter whether you went the traditional, hybrid, or self-publishing route, you should already see that you have something special.

Of course, any time you share intimate moments of your life, you may step into an uncomfortable space. Being vulnerable on the pages may cause you to shy away from ever sharing your work because *what will people think?* That vulnerability, however, is what makes you and your story real and relatable. Your authenticity and courage to share part of your life will separate you from the competition. Sure, it can be scary to put yourself out there, first on the pages of your book and then on Instagram, but you owe it to yourself and your book to try. Need a nudge? Revisit your mission. Your mission is what will get you out of bed in the morning, ready to share your message each and every day.

If marketing is not your forte, and even if marketing is your day job, doing your book marketing is challenging. It is tough to look at your own work through an objective lens. But reading this book means you are serious about getting the word out about your book and your brand, and you have realized that you cannot do it all (nor should you have to) without guidance. You also do not have to start from scratch with your marketing. Your book can become the basis of your content marketing plan that you can rinse and repeat for years to come!

DONE-FOR-YOU DISASTERS

The attraction to already done-for-you marketing makes sense. In theory, you get to check "online marketing" off your never-ending to-do list because you are led to believe that someone is taking the whole thing over for you. This is a trap that way too many authors fall into. Just because a marketing company tells you they have it covered does not mean you can ignore what they are disseminating on your behalf. I have heard way too many horror stories in which the author blindly trusted a social media manager to grow their community and post relevant content only to find that neither was happening. But the money was already spent. Not only should you be judicious in who you hire, but you also want to be keenly aware of the content they use to promote your book and brand. That is why we work closely with our clients to co-create their messaging and content marketing strategy before they ever hand it over to someone else.

NOW LET'S BREAK DOWN WHAT THE CONTENT PIECE ACTUALLY IS

Content is the information, the value, the entertainment—basically what you share with your audience—to get them to know you, like you, trust you, and ultimately want to buy from you. It is the words, pictures, graphics, and videos that you post to your social media and your website, send out in your emails, and talk about in your speeches. To sum it up, it is your message to the world. Why do you need online content? Because your message and your mission deserve to be shared with more than just the people you might see face-to-face in your neighborhood.

Let's say you own an artisanal cheese shop. We'll call it *Don't Be Cheesy Exotic Cheeses*. Customers come in with the express purpose of buying fancy cheese. They come in and smell the aromas of your exotic cheese, they ask questions, they taste samples, and then they make a purchase. Easy, right? This, as you well know, is not how the online world works. Customers cannot come in and sample things and touch and feel and ask questions that get a response from you, face-to-face, instantaneously. That means the only way for them to get to know about you and your book is from the content you put out on the internet. They can learn about your expertise, find out why you are an authority in your industry, and get a feel for your brand personality throughout your content.

There are several ways to provide content to your audience. Here are some of them:

- Blogs
- White papers
- Podcasts
- Emails
- Social media posts
- Lead magnets
- Guest blogs
- Blog platforms like Medium and Substack
- Talks you give
- LinkedIn articles and newsletters
- Recorded videos
- Live videos
- Online summits

I want to let you in on a secret: Your book is filled with tons of content that you can use for your marketing. Later on, you will discover how you can leverage this content right from the chapters you have already written.

"Traditional marketing talks at people.
Content marketing talks with them."

~ Doug Kessler

BUT WHAT ABOUT PAID ADVERTISING?

"Bro marketers"—you know, the guys lying on the hood of a fancy car with the ocean in the background, telling you that if you buy their course you, too, can be a millionaire—tout the necessity of dropping tons of money on Facebook ads and Google ads. While I do believe ads can be beneficial in the right circumstances, you can generate a community of raving fans without ads. Paying for ads without messaging that has proven effective is like throwing money away. Even if it is only eight cents per click, it all adds up.

> **So how do you get more book sales, more stages to speak on, and the like without ads or relying on hope and prayer?**

By creating and disseminating content that speaks to your ideal client. You have already written it in your book, and now your goal should be to create an online community of people who believe in you and your mission and want to be part of your magic. As *Chicken Soup for the Soul* series cocreator Jack Canfield has said: "No matter your industry or profession, everyone wants to do business with the person who 'wrote the book.'"[9] Nurturing that community does not require you to post content on five different social media sites, email your list three times a week, and go live every morning with a cup of coffee in hand. Who has that kind of time? If anything, less is more, and we will discuss how to repurpose your content effectively so that you are not spread so thin that you are not making headway anywhere.

NOW THAT YOUR BOOK IS READY TO BE PROMOTED, LET'S GET DOWN TO IT

You will need to have a content marketing plan that includes what you will be posting on social media and which social media platform(s) you will use, a regular plan for emails, and a great lead magnet that helps you grow your email list.

This book is intended to help you get those ducks in a row so that you can begin to get the right pairs of eyes on your book and your brand to grow your authority online. Be sure to check out all the bonus materials just for you at vipbookmarketing.com. You'll find even more goodies to help you market your book.

KEY TAKEAWAYS

- Content marketing is the best way to develop your "know, like, and trust" factor with your audience in the online space.

- Your content already exists in your book; you just have to leverage it.

- Book sales are a bonus; developing your authority is the goal.

- Ads have a place, but dialing in your messaging should be priority No. 1.

- Authors are expected to be their own marketers; that's why having this book will give you the strategies needed to grow your brand online.

QUESTIONS FOR REFLECTION

- What are some types of content that you have already created?

- What are some types of content that you would like to begin posting?

- How do you think your book will lend itself to creating content?

- Look at your schedule to determine what days might work for content creation and distribution.

CHAPTER 3

FINDING YOUR
DREAM AUDIENCE

When you started writing your book, who did you picture in your mind would be reading it? Was it someone you know? Someone you have never met? You from three years ago? Is it your future client or a person who is going to buy your book and then join your programs or courses?

Before you put pen to paper, you likely defined your ideal reader, and in your book, you addressed their big problem or challenge. Throughout your book, you have offered solutions to that problem. Now it is time to think bigger, beyond your "ideal" reader. There are members of the media, influencers, summit hosts, and industry experts to also consider.

If you desire to speak on stage and sell your book at the back of the room, think about the kinds of events you would want to be part of. What live events and conferences do you need to get the book to? Who will be the event planner to book you to speak at their summit? Do you want to be a guest on podcasts? You will want to determine what types of podcasts will have your ideal reader as a loyal listener. Familiarize yourself with the hosts, and do not shy away from sending them your book to introduce yourself. I would like for you to begin to think of your book as *so much more than a book*. It is your calling card, a conversation starter, and proof of your credibility, authority, and expertise. As you shift your mindset about what your book is, you will begin to see all the opportunities that lie ahead of you.

It *is* possible to write a book with one "ideal" reader in mind and realize afterward that you want to reach someone else. But that is OK. People interpret art differently, right? Song lyrics that the artist meant to be one thing might mean something completely different to you. You can create your content marketing to reach whomever you feel would best be served by your book. Once you have figured out exactly who that audience is, it is time to determine where these people are hanging out online.

A word of caution: Whenever a new social media platform comes on the scene, (Hello, Instagram's Threads), there's a frenzy around it, and authors can get carried away in the frantic energy that arises. They feel like they have to join it fast, spend a whole bunch of time on the app, grow a following quickly and become the next big thing there.

We saw that exact thing happen with the audio-only social media app Clubhouse.[10] As soon as there was some buzz in entrepreneurial circles that this was going to be the next big thing, everyone and their mother began vying for an invite to this elusive and exclusive app. (As an aside, this was a great marketing strategy on the part of the app developers because that made people want to join it even more. I'll never forget talking to Android users who went out to buy an iPad just so they could get the app and see what all the fuss was about.) As it turns out, Clubhouse was not the next big thing that erased Facebook, Instagram, and LinkedIn from existence. Sure, it theoretically offered the opportunity for anyone to have a live conversation with celebrities. But at that time, it also required hours of listening, lacked any way to record any content, and you needed other apps to connect with followers.

I admit that I got caught up in the excitement. I tried so hard to like Clubhouse and incorporate it into my marketing plan. But as a visual learner, I found myself having such difficulty remembering what was said, and I would end up tuning out if I tried to do two things at once. Eventually, I gave myself a pass and stopped spending my valuable time on the app. Are my ideal clients there? Sure they are. But also know that they are in other places too, and that if it was taking me away from the tasks at hand and I did not particularly enjoy being there, I just did not have to keep torturing myself. In the end, I felt relieved and had the chance to focus on the social apps I like, and that helped me grow my community effectively. The moral of the story is that if you are not happy on a platform, it will not serve you, even if, in theory, your ideal readers are there.

WHERE SHOULD YOU SPEND YOUR TIME?

Stick to the platforms that you enjoy, that are simple for you to understand and utilize, and that your dream readers are using too. To determine what those platforms are, first, we must spell out who they are. For example, if it is a woman aged 35 to 60 who wants a career change, I would ask you what her current career is. If you said she works in the corporate space and wants to stay there, or she is currently in corporate and wants to become an executive coach, I would say your No. 1 platform should be LinkedIn. If, however, the same woman is in her 20s and she is a life coach transitioning to business coaching, then I would say you want to be on Instagram and potentially Facebook too. In general, here are the statistics that will help you determine what platforms work best for you.

A 2021 study from the Pew Research Center finds that 70 percent of Americans ages 18 to 29 use Facebook. But Facebook users skew older: 77 percent of Americans ages 30 to 49 and 73 percent of ages 50 to 64 are on the platform. The use of Instagram, TikTok, and Snapchat is pretty common in the under-30 crowd, while Americans with higher levels of education are more likely than those with some college experience or a high school diploma or less to be LinkedIn users.[11] While many social platforms serve relatively equal numbers of men and women, Pinterest is heavily skewed toward the latter. Pinterest, however, much like YouTube, should not really be lumped in as a social media platform. Both of these services truly are search engines since users go on them to find answers, be entertained, and shop, not to connect with friends, family, or colleagues.Even when you know you are on the best platform for your book, it is vital that you keep up with any changes and familiarize yourself with best practices. When my first-ever author client and I began working together, her contract with a big advertising firm, which helped her grow her Facebook page follower count to about 10,000 people, had just ended. Sounds amazing, right? But there was a problem. Facebook has become a pay-to-play platform in many ways. Unlike back in 2008, when those who liked your Facebook business page were very likely to see your page posts, now you are required to pay money to boost a post for followers to see it. This means that unless she is willing to pay each time she posts on her page, all those followers are extremely unlikely to see the content she is putting out. Consider this a cautionary tale about why knowing the ins and outs of a platform is key. Instead of growing her following on her business page, she could have used that ad spend to grow a Facebook group. If she had done that, she would have been able to utilize the platform better to reach her community.

Use of online platforms, apps varies – sometimes widely – by demographic group

% of U.S. adults in each demographic group who say they ever use ...

	YouTube	Facebook	Instagram	Pinterest	LinkedIn	Snapchat	Twitter	WhatsApp	TikTok	Reddit	Nextdoor
Total	81	69	40	31	28	25	23	23	21	18	13
Men	82	61	36	16	31	22	25	26	17	23	10
Women	80	77	44	46	26	28	22	21	24	12	16
White	79	67	35	34	29	23	22	16	18	17	15
Black	84	74	49	35	27	26	29	23	30	17	10
Hispanic	85	72	52	18	19	31	23	46	31	14	8
Ages 18-29	95	70	71	32	30	65	42	24	48	36	5
30-49	91	77	48	34	36	24	27	30	22	22	17
50-64	83	73	29	38	33	12	18	23	14	10	16
65+	49	50	13	18	11	2	7	10	4	3	8
<$30K	75	70	35	21	12	25	12	23	22	10	6
$30K-$49,999	83	76	45	33	21	27	29	20	29	17	11
$50K-$74,999	79	61	39	29	21	29	22	19	20	20	12
$75K+	90	70	47	40	50	28	34	29	20	26	20
HS or less	70	64	30	22	10	21	14	20	21	9	4
Some college	86	71	44	36	28	32	26	16	24	20	12
College+	89	73	49	37	51	23	33	33	19	26	24
Urban	84	70	45	30	30	28	27	28	24	18	17
Suburban	81	70	41	32	33	25	23	23	20	21	14
Rural	74	67	25	34	15	18	18	9	16	10	2

Note: White and Black adults include those who report being only one race and are not Hispanic. Hispanics are of any race. Not all numerical differences between groups shown are statistically significant (e.g., there are no statistically significant differences between the shares of White, Black or Hispanic Americans who say the use Facebook). Respondents who did not give an answer are not shown.
Source: Survey of U.S. adults conducted Jan. 25-Feb. 8, 2021.
"Social Media Use in 2021"

PEW RESEARCH CENTER

Group members are more likely to see posts, and there are other benefits, like being able to ask for an email address prior to joining!

Since I did not have a time machine (and sadly, I still don't), I suggested we implement a grassroots reach out to those who "liked" the page and get them to join a Facebook group. When we started engaging with them in the DMs, and offering them a wonderful lead magnet as an incentive to join the group, it worked. But even so, we could not manage to connect with all 10,000 people. I often wonder what would have happened if she'd put all that money into growing her Facebook group instead.

Beyond the social media platform selection, something else to consider when strategizing how to reach your audience is to understand how *you* prefer to create content. For me, I could do live videos all—day—long. Recorded videos are not as much fun for me because I tend to make mistakes and then feel compelled to keep redoing it until it is perfect. But with live video, I know that the stakes are high, so I have to get it right the first time. I love to stream live on LinkedIn and Facebook, as well as YouTube. Then I know I'm reaching my audience in a way that feels good.

Please visit vipbookmarketing.com to get an exclusive breakdown of social media demographics and so much more.

TIME TO GET ENGAGED

If you want to truly get to know your ideal audience, aside from being on their preferred social platform and speaking to them in the ways they ingest content, you also want to be following them and the accounts they are following. There are plenty of ways to do this on different platforms. Regardless of whether you spend time on LinkedIn, Instagram, or TikTok, the social media apps themselves will give you suggestions of similar profiles to follow, so do some investigating and start following potentially perfect people. Then start engaging with them. Leave comments, and ask questions. If they comment on your posts, reply to those comments with more than just emojis. Start a conversation, move it to the DMs, and see where it goes.

Now go a step further. Who are your competitors? The big ones, like the Brené Browns and Gary Vaynerchuks of the world—the ones with hundreds of thousands of marketing dollars behind them. Follow them! Watch your competitors to see what they are doing and start following their more active followers. As you start to see your audience growing with the right people, you will be able to test your content to see what resonates with them. You may have 500,000 followers on Instagram, but if they are not your ideal people, they are never going to buy from you. A smaller but more engaged audience is always preferable.

KEY TAKEAWAYS

- Think about who needs to get a copy of your book: members of the media, influencers, summit hosts, and industry experts.

- Know that you are allowed to change your ideal reader avatar.

- Consider what the best use of your time on social media will be, and remember you do not have to jump on the bandwagon with each new platform if your ideal reader is not there or if it does not feel comfortable to you.

- Determine how you prefer to create content.

- Engage with your audience regularly.

QUESTIONS FOR REFLECTION

- What members of the media, influencers, summit hosts, and industry experts should read your book?

- What live events and conferences do you need to get the book to?

- Who will be the event planner to book you to speak at their summit?

- What social media platforms should you be on?

- Who are the influencers in your space to follow?

CHAPTER 4

BEWARE OF MARKETING FAILS

Have you ever been solicited in a direct message to participate in a very distant acquaintance's book launch? I have. Even if I barely know them, I think it is fun to help someone reach an important status for their hard work. Becoming an Amazon best-selling author certainly has cachet, but you should know that there is a system that you, too, can follow to become a best-selling author yourself. You can even pay beaucoup bucks to get on the bestseller lists of major publications. Once you achieve bestseller status, no one can ever take that away from you.

Your book can be guaranteed to become a bestseller. That sounds amazing, right? But whether your book is a bestseller or not, gracing that list for an hour or two is not enough to skyrocket you to stardom. Your new title (Bestselling Author) will look fabulous in your bio, but it is not going to do what we marketers insist upon, like broken records. Being a bestseller does not warm up your audience to become fans who know, like, and trust you, and who are ready to buy from you. A comprehensive book marketing plan is required.

In this chapter, I want to lay out the mistakes that people make when implementing their marketing (regardless of bestseller distinction). Ensuring that you don't fall into these traps that are as ubiquitous as cat videos on YouTube is vital. Not only will you avoid being *just like everyone else,* but you'll find that you are also fulfilling your mission as you go.

Let's jump into the three reasons content marketing fails and how you can avoid these missteps yourself.

LACK OF ORIGINALITY

Facebook is filled with posts like this: *"I made $14K in one week using this foolproof method of getting clients. Drop an emoji below to get the exact framework I used."*

Ugh. Cringe. This is what I call the Facebook marketing trap. You can, of course, substitute Facebook for Instagram or even LinkedIn, for that matter, because these predatory posts exist across platforms.

Since there are *so* many things wrong with this, I am just going to dive in. Here are my top 10 gripes about this post:

1. You have no proof that this person really made that amount of money in the time frame they said.

2. You don't know how warm those leads were.

3. You don't know whether they had multiple phone calls prior to closing these deals.

4. You don't know what they are selling.

5. You don't know whom they sold to. Maybe it was one high-ticket offer to one person.

6. You don't know whether this was a recent sale or years ago.

7. You don't know who created the method they are using.

8. You don't know whether it is American, Canadian, or Australian dollars.

9. You don't know whether this person is flat-out lying about making $14K at all.

10. You have no idea whether this method can work for you.

These posts are super enticing. It is hard to resist someone offering you the opportunity for immense success for *free*! We love silver bullets. We love taking the easy way out. Hello, diet pills and non-invasive surgical procedures to remove fat in unwanted areas. Goodbye, exercise and sticking to a healthy diet. Someone wants to give me an easy way to make lots of money, and all I have to do is drop an emoji in the comments to get it? Sign me up!

OK, time out. Please pause and think before you get stuck in this person's endless email marketing funnel. If it sounds too good to be true, you know it probably is. And yet, generic marketing plans are sold every day to unsuspecting business owners when they read the screenshots of happy client testimonials.

> **Cookie-cutter marketing plans do not work the way you are promised they will.**

Nothing can universally work for everyone. There is no way on earth they can be individualized by the creator to suit your needs specifically. But that shiny object syndrome is real! You want to get the next exciting marketing course so you can beat the competition. But it is easy to get caught in the inertia of learning, not doing, and things change in marketing so fast, rendering such programs obsolete on the regular.

What about those products that say you can just buy 365 days' worth of Instagram captions for $27, post them, and you are done? As I mentioned in chapter one, you have a unique mission with your book and your brand. Sure, your pipeline of posts will be full, but that is all it will be: full. When you buy templates you are supposed to plug and play into your marketing, it would be virtually impossible for the writer of said generic captions to capture your voice and intention.

"Failure is another stepping stone to greatness."
~ Oprah Winfrey

HOW ANNE LEARNED TO STOP BEING "GENERIC"

My client Anne had hired a company to post on her LinkedIn for several months before she came to work with me. In one of our first meetings, we spent a great deal of time scrolling through the platform to see the posts that were residing on her account. I had high hopes at first. She had plenty of posts dating back a few months, which was great because that meant there was activity. But when we started reading them out loud and really looking at the accompanying stock photos, it became exceedingly clear that these posts were painfully generic. All the photos were stock pictures, and boring ones at that—hello, random hands on a keyboard—and the captions were as generic as store-brand ice cream.

The posts were not speaking to anyone in particular, and as a result, they were talking to no one at all. Unsurprisingly, it was rare for more than one person in her network to bother to like her posts, let alone comment on them. Anne had fallen into the cookie-cutter trap, thinking that as long as posts were there, they were doing her marketing. Sure, they were taking up space, but they were not serving her in any beneficial way. In fact, they were doing her a disservice. If a potential client had come across her LinkedIn page and looked at what she was posting, there is no way they would have related to her content. When people consume your content, the silent question going through their heads is, *What is in it for me?* If there is nothing in it for them, you best believe they will keep scrolling, and that's the end of that. Now Anne has a list of more than 60 content topics tailored to her brand's specific needs that she or her social media manager can choose from. Each one is sure to call out her exact audience and speak to them—no more posting just for the sake of it.

LACK OF CLARITY

This brings me to the second reason that content marketing fails. A lack of clarity, not just in messaging but with who the ideal audience is that you need to be cultivating.

In an earlier chapter, I referenced when Clubhouse became the next big thing, and "Are you on Clubhouse?" was a common post to see while scrolling through my social media platforms. People spent hours hanging out in various rooms, hosting rooms, and talking about Clubhouse and how it was going to change social media forever because it leveled the playing field for celebrities and us regular folk. But what a lot of marketers failed to mention is that not everyone needs to jump the Facebook ship or spend 24/7 soaking up all that Clubhouse has to offer. In fact, for people like me who are strictly visual learners, Clubhouse was a pretty tough platform to get used to. The more I thought about it, the more I realized that this platform did not serve me at all, and I stopped allowing myself to feel FOMO (Fear Of

Missing Out) for not having the app open all day while I was trying to get work done.

Ask yourself, is your audience even on a particular platform? If not, do not invest your time (and money) in another social media app. If you really cannot stomach a particular platform and you feel a pit in your stomach even having to open up the app, then I am giving you full permission just to skip it. You need to be fully invested. Reluctant and miserable marketers will not spend time learning the nuances, prospecting, or doing any of the things that will ensure success on that platform.

To begin to get some good traction on your preferred social platforms, try calling out your ideal reader/customer/client. When I post on my social platforms, I often start with a hook that truly speaks to my ideal clients:

- Hey, authors!

- Are you an author?

- It's time to stop spinning your wheels and market your book the right way!

- Have you published your book?

- Have you written a book, and you do not know what to do next?

You get the picture. It is pretty clear that I am talking to you—someone who has written a book and wants to create excitement around their book and brand to sell copies, amplify their mission, speak on stages, fill programs, and so much more.

IT'S NOT JUST SEMANTICS

Language matters. You have to get the wording right. Here is an example that I've tweaked slightly for authors. It's based on what one of my mentors, Danielle Cevallos, President of Kelly

Roach International and Conviction Marketing Agency, has used. Let's say you are a fitness expert, and your book focuses on how to lose the last ten pounds that have been hanging around since having a baby (however many years ago that was) using exercises that are sure to do the trick. It is vital that you know the language that your ideal reader uses to describe their problem. If your person is so focused on getting toned arms and you are posting copy touting how your book will help them "get skinnier," then your marketing will just fall on deaf ears.

Not sure how to know what your target audience is complaining about or is struggling with? That is an easy fix. Head over to the social platform they are hanging out on and read their posts.

Here are some other ways to ensure your content is crystal clear:

- Avoid using too much jargon.
- Aim for shorter and more succinct ideas that are easy to digest on the go.
- Address a problem, then provide a solution.
- Give tips that help position you as an authority in your space.
- Make a plan. Don't just post whatever you feel like on a whim. It needs to relate back to your book and your brand.

To that last point of making a plan when you do not have one, you could fall victim to the third reason that content marketing fails: a lack of consistency.

LACK OF CONSISTENCY

Let's talk about what I call the spaghetti problem. Not only is spaghetti delicious, but it is also a great symbol of what happens to authors who take on their content marketing without first educating themselves on the dos and don'ts. Let me first say, kudos to you for taking action to do your marketing the right way by buying this book! Without a content marketing plan, whatever you post will be like throwing spaghetti at the wall to see what sticks. But we can even take this a step further. What if the spaghetti sticks, but you cannot seem to figure out why it stuck or even what brand you cooked with? How can you recreate that wonderful sticky spaghetti? How can you make that same spaghetti regularly so the people eating it can come to expect such great noodles?

OK, now that I have beaten that metaphor to death, let's unpack this.

When you create content that gets excellent engagement, it means that it resonates with your ideal audience, so you will want to make more of it. Regularly. The last part is vital. A lack of consistency is what many authors find to be their downfall when it comes to content marketing. Unfortunately, the occasional post or email is not going to be enough to nurture your audience, show them your expertise, or create a trusting relationship. If you do not show up for them, they will not show up for you. So, if you are truly invested in marketing your book and your brand, you must do it every week, rain or shine. And in the next chapter, I am going to show you exactly how to become consistent with your content marketing.

The messaging piece is something I dive into right away with clients. For more bonus content and to learn how our programs can benefit your book and brand, head over to vipbookmarketing.com.

KEY TAKEAWAYS

- Cookie-cutter marketing plans don't live up to their hype.

- A lack of clarity in messaging and who your audience is will stifle your content marketing success.

- Try calling out your ideal reader/customer/client on social media to get their immediate attention.

- Using words that your ideal audience uses will reach them in their language.

- Planning your content will ensure that your audience is served and that you are consistent with your marketing.

QUESTIONS FOR REFLECTION

- What have you been doing with your content that can be more tailored to your audience?

- What words do your ideal readers use to describe their struggles, challenges, and complaints?

- How can you make sure that your messaging is really clear to your audience?

- What can you stop doing that isn't working?

CHAPTER 5

PUTTING ON YOUR GRANNY PANTIES

I call consistency the "granny panties of marketing." Why? Because being consistent is not sexy at all, but it is necessary, and it serves an important purpose. So much of marketing is exciting: fun visuals, live collaborations on Instagram, being a featured guest on a podcast . . . But I would argue that consistency, the unsexiest part of marketing, is what truly moves the needle.

I am a bit of a control freak. I think as an entrepreneur, the desire—scratch that, intense need—to be in control often goes with the territory. You have a great idea that is *your* idea. So, of course, no one can execute that idea as well as you can, right? Well, here is the one element of your content marketing that is *completely* under your control: how reliably you show up for your community.

That means posting on your social media platform of choice each day that you have decided you are going to post. It means adhering to a schedule for your email marketing, going live, or publishing your podcast. This requires you to stick to it, prepare beforehand, and even record ahead of time. In short, it requires planning. But guess what? Being consistent will set you apart from the competition. It will help you build up the *know, like, and trust* factor. When your readers are ready to buy, they will buy from you. While everyone else posts things one time and wonders why nothing happens, you get your message out regularly, and people start to take notice. No more reinventing the wheel each time you post. You can repurpose your best work across platforms too.

> **Being consistent will set you apart from the competition.**

BUILDING CONSISTENCY INTO YOUR MARKETING

When you show up for your followers, rain or shine, you are letting them know that you are here for the long haul, you are dedicated to them, and you are not going to leave them hanging. As you continue to show up, you, your book, and your brand will begin to become top of mind for your online fans. Plus, as your community sees you putting in the effort, you will develop more of a relationship with them. They will begin to know you, like you, and trust you. When they are looking for someone who serves clients the way you do, they will be much more likely to remember you. Your consistent efforts will ultimately help grow your online reach because more people will share, comment on, and discover your great content.

"Consistency beats talent.
Consistency beats money.
Consistency beats intellect.
Consistency beats fear."

~ Jasmine Star

LEARNING TO PLAY THE GAME

If you are thinking, *But this is all free, and I don't have time to give things away for free,* we have to make a mindset adjustment right now. The truth is, to play the game, you have to give away content. You do not have to give away the cow, the milk, and everything in between, but you do need to regularly give value online. It is also human nature to reciprocate.

> **When you give your audience valuable tips and information, they are naturally going to want to buy from you in return.**

Somewhat ironically, even though I thoroughly enjoy being in control, I am not a natural at planning. It has been probably the biggest learning curve for me with my own marketing, and I have had to get really disciplined about putting everything on my calendar. There is a great line from the 1990 film *Pretty Woman* that sums me up pretty well: "I wouldn't say I'm a planner. I would say I'm a kinda fly by the seat of my pants gal. You know, moment to moment, yeah, that's me." In college, I cohosted a radio show. While my job was not to book the guests, my role as cohost was to ask questions and lead the conversation. I would regularly come huffing and puffing into the studio a few minutes before air time and begin interviews with absolutely no idea who I was talking to—literally, not a clue. Asking questions and active listening allowed me to sound good on air, and today it's what saves me, due to my allergy to intense preparation.

I greatly admire those in the travel industry as well as event planners to whom planning comes naturally. So, if it comes naturally to you, then *yay!* This will be even easier for you. If, on the other hand, you, too, suffer from the same planning affliction, this will help get you into the right mode for becoming consistent with your book marketing.

STEP 1: PLAN YOUR CONTENT

First, create a schedule that you know you will be able to adhere to. Look at your current schedule and ask yourself honestly what you can add. This is key because if you are overzealous, you run the risk of becoming overwhelmed. And when we get stuck, it is hard to push through.

Here is a sample posting schedule for an author whose ideal reader is on LinkedIn:

- Monday, post on LinkedIn.
- Tuesday, post your blog.
- Wednesday, drop a podcast episode and post it on LinkedIn.
- Thursday, send an email.
- Friday, post a newsletter on LinkedIn.

At first glance, this schedule might seem intense, but it does not have to be because you are going to plan for it! You do have the power to plan an entire quarter's worth of book marketing in advance. At the very least, planning your content a week out will give you some much-needed peace of mind so you are not frantically posting on the day of. With the plethora of planning software that allows you to pre-post your content, gone are the days of being required to post in real time. Apps like Planoly and Later will allow you to plan out your Instagram posts beautifully. You can see your grid ahead of time, plan stories, and ensure that your profile is always putting out your content. Facebook Creator Studio allows you to preplan your Facebook and Instagram simultaneously. For all-in-one planning, there are platforms like Buffer, Hootsuite, Publer, and Sendible that enable you to post on a number of different social media accounts at the same time. Just be sure that the scheduler is officially recognized by the platform so your posts are seen by your community.

No matter what time or day you post to social media or send an email, it is even *more* important that you are consistent. Every single day, we have so much noise coming at us all in our online world. When I look at my phone each morning, I have at least 200 unread emails waiting for me. It is daunting. Consistency will help you stand out in the crowd because the members of your community will come to expect to hear from you.

STEP 2: REPURPOSE YOUR CONTENT

Everything old is new again. Bell bottoms came back into style, and your previously written content can too. The goal as a marketer for your book is to avoid having to reinvent the wheel across every social media platform and everywhere else you may place your content.

Here are some strategic ways to repurpose your content to save you a lot of time and provide value to your potential clients and customers. Suppose you write a blog post (which I hope you will begin doing); you can think of that blog as the foundation for your content planning in a given week. Here are some ways to repurpose the blog post:

- When you write an email newsletter, you can use the blog post as the text of your email.

- Take your blog article and break it up into chunks that you can use as captions over the course of several days on your Instagram and Facebook.

- If you have a podcast, you can take your blog article and use that as the script for your weekly show.

- Do you post videos on YouTube? Never wonder what to say because it can be exactly what you have written in your blog post.

- Create a Pinterest pin and use it to pin a link to your blog.

- Not only can you use parts of your blog article as posts on LinkedIn, you can even post your entire blog as an article and newsletter on LinkedIn, with pictures and links.

These are all incredible ways to get your message out into the world based on *one* blog post. Let's keep going! Another way to repurpose content is by updating an old blog post and making it new again. You can add different, up-to-date information, maybe even change the title slightly. There you have a brand-new post to do all of the above with.

If you prefer to start with video content, then you can totally reverse the process. There are several platforms like Otter.ai that will transcribe your videos. Within minutes, you will have a written version of your video. A quick word of caution, though: When you first read that video, it likely will not sound as good as you thought. In order to make your blog post more coherent, you will need to do some copyediting. Once you have cleaned it up, you can take that copy and make blog posts, social media posts, Pinterest pins, and more. Another idea is to repurpose your social media posts. If you are like me, you put a great deal of thought into what you are writing on social platforms. I bet that if you scrolled through your social media feed, you could find a bunch of fabulous posts that would go together to make a pretty great newsletter. Plus, you will already have great pictures to go with it.

STEP 3: GET ACCOUNTABILITY

If you feel that you will not be able to keep it up, try finding an accountability partner or a coach who specializes in content marketing for books (hi there!). So often, we have a great plan, we know how we are going to execute it, and then something comes up, and we forget, or we get sidetracked. Somehow two weeks go by, and we have not posted on Instagram or sent an email. This is where a lot of people get stuck. They tell themselves, "I didn't do anything in the past two weeks, so I should just throw up my hands and say forget it." Instead, start again. You do not have to tell people why you fell off the wagon; you just have to get back on and keep going. We have built accountability for our clients right into our programs because it's *that* important! Head over to vipbookmarketing.com to get the details and for helpful content planning tools.

Marketing your book can be lonely and overwhelming. You deserve to have the support and accountability on a weekly basis to keep pushing through. So when your competitors forget to post and send emails, you are still going strong. You are creating that client loyalty, that know, like, and trust factor, and above all, you are being consistent.

KEY TAKEAWAYS

- Planning does not have to give you anxiety.

- Get yourself some planning software. There are several free platforms that are great.

- Consistency is key to growing your brand online.

- Do not reinvent the wheel; repurpose your content across platforms.

QUESTIONS FOR REFLECTION

- What content do you already have that you can repurpose? (Hint: your book!)

- How can you hold yourself accountable?

- What content dissemination schedule can you implement?

- What will you look at to measure your results?

CHAPTER 6

THREE SIMPLE STRATEGIES FOR SUCCESS

Let's look at the big picture: Your goal is to create and implement a book marketing strategy that attracts, resonates with, and inspires your ideal audience to take action. In general, taking action means a person joins your client journey as they get to know, like, and trust you. Step one is to download your lead magnet (freebie). Step two is to buy your book. Steps three and on are to sign up for your programs and courses, hire you in a one-to-one setting, and watch you speak on stage. This is the tried-and-true formula we use with our clients to grow their audience, build their credibility, and help them make money by leveraging their book. The secret ingredient for its success is authority-building content.

> *"A goal without a plan is just a wish."*
> ~ Antoine de Saint-Exupéry

There is no such thing as a one-size-fits-all approach to book marketing. The "$27 content calendar with 365 days' worth of posts already written for you!" is not a magic bullet. That said, there are some universal strategies you can use to guide you in creating content that is authentic to your book and brand. In this chapter, we will outline some of these approaches that you will be able to tailor to your individual audience, book, and mission.

Strategy No. 1 is all about creating marketing content using your book as the foundation. Content that highlights your expertise will help you shine as a thought leader in your field. When you provide your community with valuable information, that positions you as an expert.

Some examples of authority-building content are

- blog posts
- short e-books
- articles (on your platform or other people's platforms)
- white papers (longer and in-depth articles stating a problem and solution with stats to back up your claims)
- lead magnets
- longer social media posts

There is no better way to grow your authority than by leveraging what you have already created. Your book contains so many juicy nuggets of wisdom that you can repurpose for all your content needs. One thing to note is that it is unlikely that you will be able to copy and paste a paragraph from your book verbatim into an Instagram caption, for example. When we write books, we use long sentences, extremely verbose clauses, and way more three-syllable words than you may realize. These do not tend to work well on social media. It has nothing to do with the intelligence of your followers and everything to do with time.

> When someone is scrolling Instagram, they
> are likely doing at least one other thing
> simultaneously—watching TV, exercising, sitting
> on the toilet—so you have to account for the
> short amount of time you have to capture
> their attention.

If you have only one second to hook someone, a sentence that begins with a giant clause is not going to excite them. Their eyes will scan past it to the next thing that their busy brain can instantly comprehend. With that said, the editing required to go from book to post will be minimal.

PULLING GREAT CONTENT RIGHT FROM THE PAGES

Peruse your book for content you can pluck right from its pages. For example, you can make each chapter topic its own blog article or social media post. When you wrote your book, you were very deliberate about what you wanted to include in each chapter. You likely have some great content to pull from. If you have 12 chapters, you now have 12 ideas you can write about. Your ideas are laid out clearly in front of you in black and white. Take them and reuse them. They are yours!

Now let's flip back to the beginning of your book. Here we should find your introduction. Even if it is not as long as some of the other chapters, it is likely chock-full of heart and your wish for what your reader will get when they join your journey (a.k.a. read your book). Revisit those sentiments and consider how you can create content right from them. Did you talk about your childhood? Is there a wild or outrageous story you told? Do you have some facts that your audience will find mind-blowing or totally depressing? Pull it all and create some content.

Do you love inspirational quotes? I look at them often when I need a quick jolt back to positivity. As you may have noticed, motivational messages are sprinkled throughout this book to inspire you! If you have included any quotes from others either at the beginning of each chapter or embedded throughout your book, repurpose them. You can pepper your content calendar with those same quotes and explain their significance to you and your mission. If you have sprinkled quotes from your own brilliant mind, share those as well, since they will help establish you as an authority, not just within the pages of your book but in your marketing as well.

In almost every chapter, stories illustrating your mission are surely sitting patiently, waiting to be retold online. Whether they are client stories, client wins, or client transformations that illustrate how effective you are at what you do, or your personal stories that talk about where you have been or how you got to where you are now, these are all beautiful additions to your content lineup. We really respond to stories.

Storytelling goes back to our beginning as a human race. It is how we make sense of the world around us. And stories are the best way for us to remember things. Just think back to your high school history class. Did you have to memorize a bunch of names and dates? Was that fun or a great way to retain information? *No.* I was lucky enough to have a high school history teacher who brought history to life. Mr. Dworkin once jumped up on my desk to orate the speech of a French politician. There's nothing more memorable than that to a 15-year-old! To this day, I recall more from that class than I do from anything else I learned in high school. Your stories will resonate with your audience and make you much more memorable.

THE POWER OF THE LEAD MAGNET

Lead magnets can help position you as a thought leader. But so often, they are done *all wrong*. I could have written an entire chapter on lead magnets, but I have whittled it down considerably. Nevertheless, please hear me when I say, DO NOT GIVE AWAY THE FIRST CHAPTER OF YOUR BOOK AS YOUR LEAD MAGNET. Please do not take all caps as yelling; I'm just really fervently imploring you to stop this practice.

The reason to have a lead magnet is simple—give your ideal reader something for free that they are going to want so much that they give you their email address in exchange. Many years ago, people were not as wise as they are now about how valuable their email address is. Nowadays, you really have to give something valuable. The goal of your lead magnet is to get someone to join your customer journey. Think of this as the thing that gets them to learn about you, what you are all about, why they should want to join your community, as well as how you can help them.

> **Your freebie should provide them with a quick win—something they can accomplish today, tomorrow, or at the most, this week.**

This instantly positions you as an expert, someone who has successfully helped them with a small problem. Then they realize how great you are, start to know, like, and trust you, and what happens next? They buy your book, join your program, and more.

What happens if you offer your ideal reader the chance to download the first chapter of your book? In a word, nothing. When someone is debating whether they should give you their precious email address, they are evaluating how it will benefit them. If you offer a download of the first chapter of your book, would your ideal reader

- Get a quick win?
- See you as an expert in your industry?
- Know, like, and trust you?
- Really want to pay you so they can finish reading your book?
- Even bother reading it?

Probably not. Is your first chapter your best one? Unlikely. Will it give them quick, actionable steps to get a win? Nah. Will it show them that you are an expert and they should buy your book and then hire you to coach them? Doubt it. So please stop. The lead magnet needs to be its own entity. The thing that opens a window into the world of you and how you help your reader. It should be something that comes before the book. Not the book itself. And I am jumping off my soapbox now.

Once you have created a fabulous lead magnet (not the first chapter of your book or, heaven forbid, the table of contents, but I digress), you can use this bad boy to grow your audience exponentially. The landing page link can go everywhere—on every social media platform you have, in your email signature (not the email marketing one), when you network online and in person, and any time you are a guest on an online show or a podcast. You will see your email subscriber list begin to expand significantly. If you already have a lead magnet, how is it converting? How many downloads are you getting on a weekly basis? If the answer is *not so many*, it is time to revisit your freebie and really dive deep into what your prospective audience wants to learn from you.

Strategy No. 2 is the step *after* your lead magnet gets downloaded. It is about nurturing your audience with email marketing. An email welcome sequence—sometimes called a nurture sequence—that strategically builds the know, like, and trust factor with your prospect. In the online marketing space, there is always a big focus on generating leads. But what happens when you get those leads? If you do not follow up with them via email and usher them along your client journey, it is like having a huge bucket of leads with a hole in the bottom. That would be a terrible waste of time and money.

EVERYONE LOVES A WARM WELCOME

When you create a welcome email sequence, you are already going a step further than a lot of other brands. According to Invesp, leading experts in the conversion rate optimization industry, only 58 percent of brands send welcome emails to new subscribers, and yet, 74 percent of people are expecting that welcome email to arrive in their inbox.[12] Influencer Marketing Hub reports that a good email open rate is around 17 percent across industries, but welcome email open rates average above 80 percent![13]

With welcome emails being so vital, here is a pro tip: Make sure your freebie is only available to your prospect through email, not instantly on your landing page. This ensures that

- Your ideal reader will not grab your freebie and immediately forget about you.
- They will get used to opening emails from you.
- The next email you send, they are more likely to remember your name and not send you to the dreaded spam folder.

Now that they are opening your emails, you can provide them with amazing content that gets them primed and ready to buy your book.

Strategy No. 3 is to create long-term loyalty and real relationships with your community. Success in building your online community is partially dependent on being on the right platform where your people are hanging out. While you can create loyalty and relationships on social media, I want to focus the third strategy on email marketing as a growth tool.

> The hard truth is that you don't own your social media followers. You are parking your car in the Metaverse parking lot, and if Meta decides to tow your car . . . well, you are out of luck.

Many people remember that one fateful day in October 2021 when both Facebook and Instagram were down. But those of us who have an email subscriber list were still able to reach out to our communities. It could happen again. Yet, having a list you continually nurture will enable you to always be able to connect with your ideal readers. (Remember to periodically download your list to be safe.)

Email marketing has a multitude of benefits for your brand. Emails keep you and your book top of mind, for one thing. A whopping 99 percent of people who use email check their inbox every single day, and many of those people not only check their email up to 20 times per day, but they often check email first thing in the morning before they do anything else, according to data from OptinMonster.[14] So people are reading your emails in bed; it does not get more intimate than that. Another great thing about email is that you can see when someone received your message and whether they have read it. Social media does not come close to doing that.

LEAPING PAST THE AVERAGE RATES

When my client Sara and I began working together, we were starting from scratch to build her brand as an author of a hilarious and helpful series of children's books. Instead of a traditional how-to lead magnet, we opted for one geared toward children: a chore chart that mom (her ideal client) could print out for free for her kiddos (her ideal readers). We implemented an email nurture sequence to follow up, and Sara got to work growing her list through Instagram and Facebook. She went from never sending mass emails to having a consistent open rate of 55 percent!

That can be you too! So right now, I want you to stop and ask yourself:

- What is stopping me from sending emails on a regular basis?
- Is it the fear of sounding not smart enough?
- Am I afraid of annoying people?
- Have I simply forgotten to do it, and now I think it's too late to start sending emails again?

Let's call these thoughts out for what they are. They are just stories you have told yourself. Does the Gap worry about how many emails you have received this week? Of course not! I get an email every single day from that company.

> If someone unsubscribes from your list, then I want you to know that they are actually doing you a favor! They were not your ideal reader, and now they are not taking up valuable space on your list that could go to someone more deserving.

So, say goodbye to them and move on. Unless you are sending out emails every single day that say "BUY THIS NOW," it is highly unlikely that you are annoying your email subscribers. If you have been meaning to send emails and months have gotten away from you, it is also not too late to start again.

NOT ALL EMAILS ARE CREATED EQUAL

There are three types of emails that you, as a marketer of your book and brand, need to know: nurture emails, sales emails, and hand-raiser emails. We are going to go in-depth on each of these so you can get a feel for how they work and how they convert to readers and paying clients.

Nurture emails often get called newsletters. I believe that is a misnomer. The point of this email should not be to fill subscribers in on "what has been going on with you." Instead, the goal of a nurture email is to provide value to the recipient. Even if your whole email is about a podcast you were recently a guest on, make the email super valuable and tell the reader why listening to this podcast will benefit them. Nurture emails will warm up a cold lead, and when the time is right for them, they'll buy.

There is an appropriate time and place for a **sales email.** Just like you would not propose marriage on the first date, the sales email is vital to your marketing strategy but should not be the first thing you send.

> After you have shown your email subscribers how great you are and how much value you provide, you can feel confident encouraging them to purchase your book, your programs, speaking events, and more.

Hand-raisers are a slightly newer breed of email, but they are very effective. Often recipients will not even realize that this email is not a private email from you until they scroll down to the bottom and see that it has been sent from a mailing list. In these emails, you call out a specific group of people, encourage them to join a program or an event, tell them exactly what's in it for them, and end with a simple call to action. Hand-raisers also work fantastically as social media posts.

Now that you know how to weave email marketing into your book marketing strategy, in the next chapter, we are going to spend time on social media marketing for your book. Be sure to visit vipbookmarketing.com to get a special bonus on how to write email subjects lines that get noticed.

KEY TAKEAWAYS

- Done-for-you content costing only $27 will not be as effective as you hope.

- When you tell stories about your past and how you've helped transform the lives of others, you are being your best marketer.

- You can pluck content right out of your book to create amazing and relevant content.

- Do not give away the first chapter of your book as your lead magnet. Instead, think about what can give your ideal reader a quick win and an introduction to your work.

- When you send out a welcome email, you are doing better than more than half of all brands.

- Email marketing is a great way to nurture your audience and grow loyalty without having to worry that you might be cut off one day.

- The three types of emails to implement are nurture emails, sales emails, and hand-raisers.

QUESTIONS FOR REFLECTION

- What's been stopping you from sending emails to your list?

- What type of emails do you feel good about sending out to subscribers?

- How can you begin to implement email marketing into your overall book marketing strategy?

- In what ways can you start engaging more with your audience?

CHAPTER 7

GET SOCIAL ON SOCIAL MEDIA

Y ou have likely heard of brands that grew their social media following almost overnight, and now they sell millions of dollars' worth of whatever, and all their revenue comes from social media. This is *not* the norm. It is unlikely that a social network will be the answer to all your prayers. Instead, I would like you to approach social media in a different way. Think of your platform(s) of choice as a place for you to market your book and brand. Not necessarily the place where you will make sales. The marketing rule of seven, which states that it takes seven customer touchpoints before a person will purchase from a brand, has effectively gone out the window. It is closer to 20 these days. But social media can help you connect with your audience multiple times in multiple ways to get them closer to the sale.

> You can build an audience of raving fans. Just remember that every overnight success was years in the making

Each platform has done a great service for you by gathering your ideal readers in one place. It has also provided you with analytics to determine so much about these people, including their buying behaviors. #Winning. And these folks are regulars! It's not as if they tried out LinkedIn for a few days and they are planning to move on to another app. They are here to stay. They may even be slightly addicted to the scroll. #Winningagain.

Sometimes authors are so used to being "lurkers" on social media that it takes time to get used to posting regularly. Every weekday for months, my client Mike would read and comment on his connections' posts, but he never dared to publish his own content. He was unsure of what to say, how to say it, or whether people would even take notice. In our work together, we crafted a marketing strategy using his book as the foundation for his business to help him step into thought leadership. Mike began posting some of his valuable content on LinkedIn, commenting effectively, and implementing an engagement strategy to grow his audience. Within a few weeks, he began receiving direct messages from his connections on the platform. They saw he had a book and wanted him to speak at their events. And these were paid gigs!

I often get asked, "What days should I post to (insert social media platform), and what time?" You may not like my answer. It truly depends on when your target audience is spending time online. For example, parents might be more likely to check social media when they first wake up in the morning, around dinner time, or later at night. Those in the C-suite may be on LinkedIn when they are drinking their morning coffee or before they end their workday. Instagram rewards you for more posts in a day, while LinkedIn, on the other hand, is said to give preferential treatment to profiles with only one post per day. You can take a look at the analytics of your social media profile to see when your people are most likely to see what you are posting. A quick Google search will also turn up best practices for your particular social media platform, and often the app itself will tell you what the algorithm wants.

Now, the next most-asked question is, *what should I be posting?* The short answer: all the content you can pull out of your book. Here is a broad list of different kinds of posts you can offer your audience:

Social proof. What is better than reader or client testimonials to show your social media followers that you are good at what you do? Nothing. So please do this regularly.

Case studies. Did your client do something amazing after working with you? Has your book helped people? Give your audience stories of client transformations so they can see themselves in these stories and want to work with you.

Shareable content. You can create something shareable, even if you did not say it initially. For example, if you have an inspirational quote that you love, create a graphic with it and post it. Put the photo of the person who said it in your graphic and get their followers excited too. You can also create posts with great tips for your audience and invite them to save and share the post.

Educational content. Teach your audience something new! Share a lesson you learned from a mentor or coach that changed your life.

Giveaways. You can participate in a group giveaway or create your own in which you give away your time, your services, or your book.

Authority-building posts. You have great experience in your industry. Show your audience that you are an authority in your space by offering information about your topic of choice that they would not get anywhere else.

"Getting to know you" posts. These often begin with "There are a bunch of new people here, so I wanted to introduce myself again." These posts often fare very well because people are fascinated to get a glimpse of you behind the scenes. Feel free to go TMI or keep it as superficial as you like. Just be authentically you.

Posts that inspire engagement. Remember those hand-raisers we talked about in the last chapter? They work great on social media too. Thoughtful questions also work well. You can even create a post calling out those who only lurk and inviting them to say hello in the comments.

Your why and/or your mission. Do not underestimate the importance of this. When you enroll your audience in your mission and give them a clear understanding of the reason you have written your book, they are likely to be moved to purchase it, or at the very least, to pay more attention to your posts.

Invitations to download your lead magnet. Posting about your lead magnet one time is not going to help you get lots of email subscribers. Add it to your posting rotation and remind your audience about it at least once a week.

The sale. You are welcome to ask for the sale on social media as long as that is not the only thing you do. If you have a flash sale, or you are opening or closing a cart for a program, go ahead and let your audience know.

No doubt you will come up with even more ideas of what would make a great post as you go. There really are no wrong answers, as long as what you are posting resonates with your audience. Remember, though, how you write your copy will make a difference. Not to be a member of the grammar police or anything (totally a member over here), but grammar and spelling should not be an afterthought. The occasional typo is not a big deal but a complete disregard for the English language is a no-no.

"'Build it, and they will come' only works in the movies.
Social Media is a 'build it, nurture it, engage them,
and they may come and stay.'"

~ Seth Godin

Here is a quick overview of the kind of copy that converts in the online space. Good copy speaks to your ideal client using their own words. It addresses their pain, struggles, and challenges in a way that shows you just get them. It shows them you have a solution to their problem and what's been keeping them up at night. It inspires action, elicits emotion, or does both. The old saying goes, "A picture is worth a thousand words," and you want to be able to paint a picture with your copy.

Whenever you sit down to write marketing copy, remember to make it about the reader or client in some way. Heck, even your About page on your website should not be entirely about you. The rule of thumb for a social media post is to follow some semblance of the order below:

- Begin with a hook (a story, statement, or question).
- Talk about the problem your reader is having.
- Show them you understand and that you have the solution they need.
- End with a short summary of your post and a call to action.

Even if you simply tell a story and end with a call to action that asks your audience to drop an emoji in the comments, that can be enough. But there is one more thing to note. When trying to find a good balance between providing value in the form of tips, how-tos, and selling in a post or email, I always adhere to the 80/20 rule. In general, that means 80 percent of the time I'm giving value, while 20 percent of the time, I am selling. But selling does not have to look as if it is an infomercial where . . . *but wait, if you buy one right now, you'll get another one for free; just pay shipping and handling.* Yeah, no thanks. "Selling" online really means letting people know what you offer and how you can best help and guide them. Selling is serving. You can use case studies and testimonials that show reader transformations with a call to action that asks for the book sale.

As you put in the time on your socials, you will begin to develop a trusted brand and an audience of raving fans. At vipbookmarketing.com you can grab bonus material to help you amplify your authority on social media.

KEY TAKEAWAYS

- You can help social media platforms work for you.

- Do not get frustrated if you are not making sales directly from social media. Instead, think of the platform as a great way to reach your audience every day.

- Copy that converts addresses your ideal reader's challenges, offers a solution, and gives a call to action.

- Use the 80/20 rule with sales posts on social media.

QUESTIONS FOR REFLECTION

- How can you implement social media into your overall marketing strategy?

- What kinds of posts feel right for you?

- What are some ways that you can sell on social media without feeling like a used car salesman?

CHAPTER 8

YOUR NAME IN LIGHTS

W hile this book is not about publicity per se, as an author, you need to know what public relations (PR) is, what it is not, when to do it, how it benefits you, and how it can enhance your book promotion efforts. As I've mentioned, my first job out of college was in personal PR for celebrities, where I worked on getting comedians on morning radio shows and in local newspapers to promote gigs, walked umpteen red carpets for movie premieres, and even helped throw a big celeb-attended charity event.

Broadly speaking, PR involves hiring a publicist to pitch you to various mainstream media outlets—television, newspapers, radio, online publications, and the like. The great thing about PR is that you get to be featured on other people's platforms. (You down with OPP?) You may be quoted in interviews or invited to contribute an article, possibly for a fee. There are a lot of pay-to-play opportunities. Many local morning shows will feature *anything* as long as it's paid for. In May 2021, HBO's John Oliver did a segment where he and his staff promoted a phony sexual wellness blanket, which they dubbed Venus Veil, on three different ABC-owned morning shows. The blanket was nothing more than a blanket, but the show hosts dutifully read the talking points about how effective it was. And viewers believed it. While this story is hilarious to watch, it is also a real eye-opener about what we take at face value in the media.[15]

With the news outlets you do not pay for, your publicist may not have a ton of control. Each outlet gets to decide whether you are a good fit for them. If you have a well-connected PR representative, they will have established relationships with the media and be able to call upon those to potentially get you on. When selecting a PR firm for you and your needs, it is a good idea to ask what outlets their clients have been featured in, what kind of relationships the PR professional has with those outlets, and what the timeline to potentially get you on a specific outlet looks like. Just like in marketing, there are no guarantees in PR. You will pay a monthly retainer or perhaps a lump sum upfront to a publicist, who will then create a PR plan for you. They will write media releases and put together a media kit that contains clips of where else you have been featured on mainstream media, along with a bio and book information.

"Publicity can be terrible. But only if you don't have any."

~ Jane Russell

As a book marketing strategist for nonfiction and children's book authors, I help those authors develop their marketing foundation and show them how to get their own publicity. The bridge I'm building takes you from *unknown author to impactful authority* in your industry, and it is buttressed by messaging that resonates (which is based on your book and your mission), your online presence, and your book marketing strategy as a whole. In our programs, we work with authors to help them build a business and a brand with their book as the foundation and collaborate to create timely pitches for podcasts, speaking, and media attention because authors can absolutely do their own PR.

You can pitch yourself to every outlet in the world, but even a crystal ball cannot determine whether your story will be picked up or not. It is up to the individual outlet. One thing that will give you a leg up is to tie the launch of your book into something timely.

When Suzanne launched her book about the many mental health struggles women have, we knew that while it was definitely exciting to us that her book was finally published, that would not have been enough of a reason to get mentioned by media outlets. So, we tied in Olympic athlete Simone Biles's decision to focus on her mental health and take a step back from the 2021 Summer Olympics as proof that people are talking about helping women step into their power and take back their emotional health. Sure enough, she got some great press coverage.

There's a reason that we build up to the PR piece after developing the marketing foundation. The following story will illustrate what I mean. A woman was once referred to me by mutual friends who thought she could use my help. (Spoiler alert: She really could have used it.) Her situation was this: She had hired a publicist who had been working with her for the entire year prior to our meeting. This publicist had clearly done a fantastic job, as this woman had appeared on multiple media outlets, including a national morning show. However, when I asked her how many books she had sold to date, the answer surprised me. *She had only sold one hundred books in an entire year!* That was a big red flag waving furiously in the wind for me. I immediately checked out her website and social media accounts, and as I thought, I was instantly able to diagnose the problem. It all went back to her messaging. Her book was about one topic, but her messaging across her online platforms and her website was so painfully vague that it was unclear what her book and her brand were about. When people are confused, they do not buy. And that is exactly what happened. In her case, no matter how much publicity she would get, it could not help her sell books or grow her influence.

A PLAN FOR PUBLIC RELATIONS

While it is a great way to leverage other people's audiences, it is best to implement a PR plan after you have established, clear messaging and have begun to grow an audience. Once you have these things in place, you can reap some of its benefits:

- Credibility: You will be able to splash media outlet logos across your website and throughout all your marketing to show people that *real news* takes you seriously.

- Potential for great exposure: You have the potential to be seen by millions of eyes depending on the outlet that features you and your book.

- Possible regular gig: If you wow them, the media outlet may want you to become a regular expert, which would enable you to have even more exposure to their huge audience.

All that sounds amazing, right? Hobnobbing with Hoda and Jenna would not be too shabby. How about chatting with Bill Maher or being featured on Jimmy Kimmel? Here is something to consider, though. There are no guarantees that people will buy your book after catching a minute-long TV segment about you. They will first want to investigate you further. Who are you? What is your book really about? What is the title again because they totally forget? What do you stand for? Does your mission align with their values and what they want to read right now? So, they head over to where they usually look up things—Instagram, Google, LinkedIn, etc. If you do not have an effective social presence and/or what they find does not instill confidence that you really are a subject matter expert, they close the browser or forget the search and start scrolling for other things that interest them. Then you have lost them. Possibly forever.

So how can you make sure that you have the online foundation needed to make PR as effective as possible? By following the guidance in this book and making sure you have checked out all the resources available to you.

> At the bare minimum, authors should have a landing page, a lead magnet, and a vibrant existence on social media. Think of this as your author platform.

How and where you show up online with intention is important. Meaning, you do not join TikTok because your daughter told you to, or you do not just post to LinkedIn occasionally when someone reminds you it is a good place to find new readers or clients. Instead, you have a website dedicated to you, your brand, and your book. You are on particular social media platforms by design. You have a robust email marketing strategy. You may have a podcast as part of your marketing plan. You are highlighting your expertise each day to grow your online community with your ideal audience.

Creating your online presence—the author platform—that generates leads and establishes your influence is not something you accomplish over a weekend. That's why you can start before your book is ever published. In fact, the moment you have an outline for your book, you can and should start creating a content strategy. Until your book is published and available to all (or at least, advance copies are available), you may find some challenges landing significant PR. Often, traditional media outlets will want to have a physical copy of the book prior to your interview.

THE NONNEGOTIABLE PIECE

Now is when I stand firm and put my stake in the ground. You 100 percent, hands down, need to have an author platform if you want to be regarded as a subject matter expert. When you create messaging that resonates with your ideal reader, it aids them in getting to know, like, and trust you, and helps them decide whether your personality and your book and brand resonate with them. Plus, if you are interested in getting a book deal with a traditional publisher, they will want to see that you already have excited fans. Your author platform can ultimately have an impact on your options for publishing.

PODCASTS: MARKETING OR PUBLICITY?

Podcasts live in the online space. Anyone can buy a microphone and start their own show. Podcasts are often not beholden to a network, shareholders, and advertisers. That makes it a much more level playing field. Because of this, I think that podcast guesting falls under your marketing strategy and not a publicity plan. You can certainly hire PR people who will reach out to podcast hosts and producers and pitch their clients. But I believe that podcast guesting is a tool that you can implement yourself with a bit of guidance. That's why I help my clients create their speaker one-sheet and pitch letter, along with how to find and pitch themselves to appropriate podcasts.

THE SKINNY ON PODCAST HOSTS AND PRODUCERS

Unlike a late-night comedy show on one of the big networks, which has a dedicated team of producers who are highly unlikely to entertain pitches from non-PR folk, podcast hosts and producers are much more accessible. You can easily look up their contact information right on Apple podcasts and send an email.

If you do enough research as to whether or not they take guests and whether you'd be a good fit, chances are you will at least get a reply.

The benefits of being a podcast guest are many:

- You create great content you can use in your marketing across online platforms.
- You gain credibility as an expert in your field.
- Fantastic networking opportunities exist when you establish a good rapport with the podcast host.

When my client Kristina and I started collaborating on a marketing strategy for her book series, we determined that being a guest on podcasts would be an important piece of the marketing plan so that she could leverage other people's platforms to grow her audience. Together, we designed her speaker one-sheet and crafted a pitch letter to send to podcast hosts. She has now been a guest on dozens of podcasts in her niche, and hosts are even reaching out to her to be a guest on their shows.

Like Kristina, your opportunities are endless. It just takes some strategic planning and clear messaging, which you are now well on your way to creating. For bonus content on pitching yourself to podcasts, head to vipbookmarketing.com.

KEY TAKEAWAYS

- PR can provide you with great opportunities to leverage other people's platforms and audiences.

- A great PR placement can give you credibility as an author.

- If you choose to hire a publicist, select one who is well connected in the industry and has access to the media outlets you want to be on.

- Publicity may be a lot less effective if you don't have an author platform already in place.

- Podcasting should be part of your book marketing strategy.

QUESTIONS FOR REFLECTION

- What are your goals for your book? Do you want to sell a million copies? Do you want this to be your calling card for your business?

- At what point in your marketing process would you consider hiring a publicist?

- What podcasts do you listen to that would be great to be a guest on?

- How could you make yourself stand out from the other pitches that podcast producers receive?

CHAPTER 9

THE THOUGHT LEADER'S MARKETING MINDSET

Throughout these pages, you will find lots of book marketing strategies and tactics—what to do, what not to do, and everything in between. But in this chapter, I want to discuss why your mindset around marketing is key. I can give you all the strategies in the world, but without the right mindset, you may get stuck at the starting line. *So how do you get yourself into the mindset to market your book?*

First, you have to acknowledge that you have a particular skill set that is entirely unique to you. No one else in the world can do what you do because they have not had your life experiences or specific training. You may consider some to be competition because they have published a book on a similar topic. But there is no way that they can share your individual mission, and they certainly have not experienced life the way you have.

> **Your stories—what really makes your book come alive—can never be replicated by another author.**

No one can do exactly what you do. You should not deprive the world of your book and your mission. And if no one knows about your book, you'll be doing just that.

When authors come to me with personal concerns about their online marketing, we spend as much time as necessary working through those feelings because these can make or break your ability to promote your book.

"Instead of worrying about what you cannot control, shift your energy to what you can create."
~ Roy T. Bennett

HOW TO GET OVER YOURSELF

My client Andrea wrote a book that lays out her proprietary framework for navigating life's challenges, which will undoubtedly help every reader feel empowered to handle stress and change in a healthy way. After she secured a traditional publisher and was ready to build her author platform, we determined that it would be ideal to build a robust Instagram presence. Her concern? Posting pictures of herself online. She did not want to be viewed as narcissistic or full of herself if she posted photos of her face. She did not yet accept why people would want to see pictures of her online.

At the beginning of our time together, the only picture Andrea approved of posting was her author photo. But, as I told her, posting that picture over and over would not help create the know, like, and trust factor with her followers. Instagram is an extremely visual medium. It requires new lifestyle photos (and increasingly more and more video) all the time, not one single posed picture that is more fitting for the book jacket than social media. You, the author, become the face of your brand in most cases. As such, you want to post pictures of yourself in your online marketing. People want to see you and find out what you are all about, no matter what kind of business you are in. Humans need to see faces in order to feel a connection. We need to see people doing things that we relate to in order to stop and pay attention. When you give your audience something to aspire to be, you will help draw them in.

As I helped Andrea move past her concerns, she hired a photographer to do a photoshoot for her on the streets of San Francisco. She now regularly posts photos and videos showing her face. After acknowledging the value of being the face of her brand, she has not looked back. And her followers love her posts!

MARKETING YOURSELF ONLINE MEANS REALLY PUTTING YOURSELF OUT THERE

While you get to decide how much personal information you divulge (I definitely veer toward TMI at times), you may have a number of beliefs preventing you from jumping fully into marketing your book. Have any of these negative thoughts run through your head lately?

- I never know what to say online.
- I'm worried my words will not resonate with anyone.
- What if I annoy people?
- I am afraid I will waste people's time.
- The perfectionism struggle is real: if it's not perfect, it is not good enough to share.
- I do not have meaningful content.
- Nobody is going to care.
- I find this tedious, boring, and, frankly, a waste of time.
- I do not want to seem pushy or needy.
- I'm overwhelmed and cannot figure out how to stand out.

You are not the first one to think any of these thoughts. This is an actual list I have compiled from real authors in workshops I have held who were concerned about promoting themselves in the online space. But I can easily dispel each one. Here goes: If you never know what to say online, you are in luck. Your book houses a treasure trove of things to say. If you are worried your words will not resonate, have someone you know who could be your ideal reader, read your book. They will let you know whether your words resonate.

The online space is such a crowded, noisy place that you would really have to send out oodles of emails or tag the same people over and over in your social media posts to even begin to annoy people. If you have an important message to convey, you will be adding value, not irritating people. It is very noble of you to be concerned about other people's time, but you have no control over how they spend it. If they read your email, that is their prerogative, and you do not have to attach any feelings to that. The perfectionism struggle is absolutely real, but done is *always* better than perfect. If you think you do not have meaningful content, how did you write a whole book? You do have something meaningful to say. So please say it. If nobody cares, I bet you are just speaking to the wrong people. Go ahead and find your crew. I know they are out there. If you find this tedious, boring, and frankly a waste of time, you can hire someone to do it for you once you have implemented your book marketing plan. Afraid to seem pushy or needy? I feel you. Sometimes authors think social media is a place to stand and shout over and over again about how great their book is. That is a major turnoff. But you know what is not? When you explain the value that your book will bring to your ideal reader's life. So do that instead.

Last, but certainly not least, if you do not know how to stand out, here are three things to try:

- Make sure your messaging really hits home with your audience.

- Be consistent with your content marketing. Stop posting sporadically. Show up regularly. Once you start to feel like a broken record, you will see that people begin to notice. Remember those granny panties?

- Provide tips, tell stories, and be authentically you. Those things will always make you stand out when you give of yourself to your audience.

HOW A MISSION KEEPS YOU GOING

These three methods have certainly worked for my client Crystal. When she joined our program, she had so many irons in the fire. She was finishing writing a book, developing a subscription box, working on a signature talk, and starting a podcast all at once. Plus, she had a full-time job, a child at home, and another one on the way. It is amazing that she found time to sleep! But her mission keeps her going. Her sister tragically took her own life, and since then, Crystal has felt called to devote her life to supporting people who have lost loved ones to suicide and working to highlight suicide prevention. Her goal was well defined, but she wanted guidance on how to create messaging that would spark engagement and change. So together, we crafted a content marketing strategy that would speak to her ideal readers. Crystal began blogging weekly and repurposing her blogs into social media posts and email newsletters. But like many authors, she needed that support to get started and to keep going. While she was very clear on her vision and whom she wanted to help, marketing her work and her company was not second nature. Now, she is growing her community every day and has positioned herself as a thought leader in this space. People regularly reach out to Crystal when they need an expert to speak on suicide prevention, and she's making a difference in so many lives.

Since I am not right next to you to support and advocate for you, here is an exercise you can do to help you create content that will be meaningful to your audience.

Step one: Close your eyes and picture the one person you are speaking to.

Step two: Ask yourself, what is troubling them? How are they feeling right now? How can you best serve them? How can you solve their problem? What do they need to hear from you?

Step three: Open your eyes and start to write from your heart.

Often people forget that the only medium that is really one-to-many is television. We gather around the TV to watch *Dancing with the Stars.* But with podcasts, social media, email, and YouTube videos, people don't sit around in a group listening, watching, or reading. These are individual activities. So, it is important to focus on that one member of your audience with your message. This is how you create content that will resonate with your ideal reader. So go ahead and show people how their life could be better with your help!

At vipbookmarketing.com, we've got some amazing suggestions for further reading and so much more. Check it out!

KEY TAKEAWAYS

- You are not alone in your concerns about online marketing, but you do have the power to push past them.

- Your unique skill set, as well as your life and work experiences, can never be replicated by anyone else.

- Your book and your mission deserve to be shared with the people you can help across the world.

- Always make sure your messaging really hits home with your audience.

- Be consistent with your content marketing. Don't start and stop or post sporadically. Show up regularly. Once you start to feel like a broken record, you'll see that people start to notice.

- Provide tips, tell stories, and be authentically you. Those things will always make you stand out when you give of yourself to your audience.

QUESTIONS FOR REFLECTION

- What makes you and your experience unique?

- What are some stories you have been telling yourself about online marketing?

- Why does the world deserve to have access to your book and mission?

- How can you refine your messaging and show up consistently, starting now?

CHAPTER 10

LET'S DREAM BIG TOGETHER

With the marketing skills you have acquired reading this book, you now have a toolbox filled with tools you can implement to grow your audience and get your book out to the world. You do not have to be like the hundreds of thousands of authors whose books sit on a shelf collecting dust because they never bothered to do the marketing. Let's take a moment to envision where you want to be as a result of stepping into authorship.

> **It is time to dream about your book's potential.
> The only limit to the success of your book is
> your willingness to market it.**

Here are some ideas to get you started:

Your book is the foundation for an online course. If you look back through your chapter topics, can you see the modules starting to take shape? Through this program, you share your message with so many people and truly help them transform their lives.

Your book gets you invited to be a guest on podcasts. Podcast hosts love being able to give their listeners value. Not only can they ask you about the book, but they can direct their listeners to purchase it. Podcasts are evergreen, meaning listeners will catch your episode years later and still get excited about your book.

Your book opens the door to speaking on stage. As a bona fide subject matter expert, you command a room. Then you sell books at the back of the room or provide your book as a gift to the attendees who are excited to work with you.

Your book gets you featured in the media. You have a press release that shows how timely your book is, and your expertise is so needed. You are quoted in articles and interviewed on TV as an authority in your field.

Your book is part of a subscription box. The company buys multiple copies of your book to send to thousands of new customers each month.

Your book is purchased in bulk by a corporate sponsor. A large company wants to share your message with its entire staff across continents.

What other scenarios have you imagined for your book? This is a good time to think outside the box. Maybe you want to do book signings, make library appearances, or host a summit. Write all your ideas down and visualize them taking place. These are all possible for you when you build a strong marketing foundation for your book and brand. If you are ready for more support, I invite you to connect with me to explore how we can market your book together. At vipbookmarketing.com, you will find the ways we can partner together, as well as tons of bonus materials.

PS: Take a picture of yourself with this book *and* yours and tag me on social media to be featured.

Facebook: https://www.facebook.com/vipbookmarketing
Instagram: https://www.instagram.com/vipbookmarketing
LinkedIn: https://www.linkedin.com/in/melanie-herschorn
YouTube: https://www.youtube.com/@vipbookmarketing

KEY TAKEAWAYS

- You can leverage your book to
  - Create a paid program
  - Guest on podcasts
  - Speak on stages
  - Garner media exposure
  - Join a subscription box
  - Get corporate sales and clients

QUESTIONS FOR REFLECTION

- What will your online course look like?

- What podcasts do you wish to be a guest on?

- Where do you envision yourself speaking on stage?

- What are your dream media outlets to be featured on?

AUTHOR NOTES

I am so honored that you have spent this time with me to discover how you can transform from an unknown author to an impactful authority. My passion is to help amplify authors' voices so that, together, we can help make this world a better place.

Your book's success is important to me. Your mission and message deserve to be shared. I truly hope that you are filled with excitement for all the opportunities and possibilities that marketing your book will afford you.

Be sure to download your copy of the *Ultimate Book Marketing Checklist* to ensure you are creating a comprehensive plan. Head to vipbookmarketing.com/checklist.

To book your complimentary clarity call with me, use this link: vipbook.marketing/claritycall.

Please feel free to reach out to me personally too. My email is melanie@vipbookmarketing.com. I look forward to learning about you and your book!

I am thrilled to be alongside you on your book marketing journey. Cheers to you!

GRATITUDE

It takes a village to raise a child, and it took my village for this book to be born. I would like to thank the incredible team who has helped me make it happen: Dino Marino for your cover design skills, Karen Hunsanger for your editing magic and for making me feel like a great writer, Catherine Turner for your keen proofreading, and Susie Schaefer for helping me get this baby published. Thank you, as well, to Honorée Corder for being a true inspiration.

To my wonderful, brilliant clients, past and present, who are my "why": Andrea Mein DeWitt, Crystal Partney, Kim Costa, Kristina Lucia Pezza, Lynsi Eastburn, Sara Lin, Jim Schneider, Michael Ross, Laurie B. Timms, Anne, and many more, it is an honor to be on your book marketing journey with you.

I want to acknowledge my cheerleaders and support system throughout the writing and publishing process: M. Shannon Hernandez, Ashleigh Henry, Agathe Daskalides, Aleasha Bahr, Charity Majors, and Karianne Munstedt.

To Mr. Ihor Pelech, of blessed memory: I wish I could find the words to adequately express the profound impact you had on my life, my writing, my grammar, my confidence, and ultimately my career. Thank you for challenging me to reach my full potential.

To my grandma, my parents, and my sisters, thank you for your love and support across the continent. Thank you to my dear friends who are also my family.

Thank you to my husband, Evan, for your support and unconditional love. And to my children, Deanna and Nicholas, who are my raison d'être and who also keep asking: "When are you finally going to be a published author, Mommy?" The answer is, "Now!"

ENDNOTES

1   Denise Brosseau, "What Is a Thought Leader?," Thought Leadership Lab, accessed July 18, 2023, https://thoughtleadershiplab.com/what-is-a-thought-leader.

2   Malcolm Gladwell, Outliers: The Story of Success (Boston: Little, Brown And Company, 2008).

3   Simon Sinek, *Start with Why: How Great Leaders Inspire Everyone to Take Action* (2009; repr., New York: Portfolio/Penguin, 2011).

4   Adam Eley, "*How Has IVF Developed since the First 'Test-Tube Baby'?,*" BBC News, July 23, 2015, https://www.bbc.com/news/health-33599353.

5   Denise Duffield-Thomas, *Get Rich, Lucky Bitch! Release Your Money Blocks and Live a First-Class Life* (London: Hay House UK, 2018).

6   Steven Piersanti, "The 10 Awful Truths about Book Publishing," ideas.bkconnection.com, accessed July 25, 2023, https://ideas.bkconnection.com/10-awful-truths-about-publishing.

7   BJ Gallagher, "The Ten Awful Truths - and the TenWonderful Truths -- about Book Publishing," HuffPost, April 5, 2012, https://www.huffpost.com/entry/book-publishing_b_1394159.

8   Sharon Zink, "97% of Writers Never Finish Their Novels: Here's Why," Sharon Zink, May 23, 2017, http://sharonzink.com/writing-tips/97-of-writers-never-finish-their-novels-heres-why/.

9   Jack Canfield, "Write a Book and Get It Published - Strategies for Getting Started," Jack Canfield, February 19, 2014, https://jackcanfield.com/blog/write-a-book.

10   Falon Fatemi, "The Rise and Fall of Social Audio Will Continue to Impact the Entertainment Industry for the next Generation," Forbes, February 10, 2022, https://www.forbes.com/sites/falonfatemi/2022/02/10/the-rise-and-fall-of-social-audio-will-continue-to-impact-the-entertainment-industry-for-the-next-genera-tion/?sh=11a490b75c9f.

11   Brooke Auxier and Monica Anderson, "Social Media Use in 2021," Pew Research Center, April 7, 2021, https://www.pewresearch.org/internet/2021/04/07/social-media-use-in-2021.

12   Lisa Ross, "Why Welcome Emails Are Important – Statistics and Trends [Infographic]," Invesp, updated on April 25, 2022, https://www.invespcro.com/blog/welcome-emails.

13   Jacinda Santora, "Average Email Open Rates by Industry 2023," Influencer Marketing Hub, updated on March 21, 2023, https://influencermarketinghub.com/email-open-rates..

14   Jacinda Santora, "Is Email Marketing Dead? Statistics Say: Not a Chance.," OptinMonster, August 14, 2020, https://optinmonster.com/is-email-marketing-dead-heres-what-the-statistics-show.

15   Matthew Dessem, "John Oliver Tricked Local News Shows into Promoting a Bogus 'Sexual Wellness Blanket' He Invented," Slate, May 24, 2021, https://slate.com/culture/2021/05/last-week-tonight-john-oliver-sponsored-content-sexual-wellness-blanket.html.

ABOUT THE AUTHOR

I'M MELANIE HERSCHORN
AUTHOR
BOOK ENTHUSIAST
BOOK MARKETER

Melanie Herschorn is a book marketing strategist for nonfiction and children's book authors who want to build a business with their book as the foundation. Her clients are coaches, consultants, and experts, worldwide, who have written a book and want to amplify their message and authority.

With her comprehensive background as a celebrity publicist, award-winning journalist in radio, print & TV, as well as clothing designer and entrepreneur, Melanie is uniquely positioned to support authors to develop their online presence, build a vibrant audience, step into thought leadership, and make a big impact with their book. She earned a master's degree in journalism from the Annenberg School for Communication and Journalism at the University of Southern California where she graduated first in her class.

Melanie grew up in Canada, has lived on both US coasts, and now resides in Arizona with her husband, daughter and son, her Cavalier King Charles spaniel, Marty McDog, and her Siberian cat, Phoebe.